CHANGE STARTS With ME

Talking About Race in the Elementary Classroom

MADELEINE ROGIN

Solution Tree | Press
a division of Solution Tree

555 North Morton Street
Bloomington, IN 47404
800.733.6786 (toll free) / 812.336.7700
FAX: 812.336.7790

email: info@SolutionTree.com
SolutionTree.com

Visit **go.SolutionTree.com/diversityandequity** to download the free reproducible in this book.

Printed in the United States of America

FSC
www.fsc.org
MIX
Paper from responsible sources
FSC® C011935

Library of Congress Cataloging-in-Publication Data

Names: Rogin, Madeleine, author.
Title: Change starts with me : talking about race in the elementary classroom / Madeleine Rogin.
Description: Bloomington, IN : Solution Tree Press, [2022] | Includes bibliographical references and index.
Identifiers: LCCN 2022001824 (print) | LCCN 2022001825 (ebook) | ISBN 9781952812774 (Paperback) | ISBN 9781952812781 (ebook)
Subjects: LCSH: Racism--Study and teaching (Elementary) | Race--Study and teaching (Elementary)
Classification: LCC HT1506 .R54 2022 (print) | LCC HT1506 (ebook) | DDC 305.80071--dc23/eng/20220224
LC record available at https://lccn.loc.gov/2022001824
LC ebook record available at https://lccn.loc.gov/2022001825

Solution Tree
Jeffrey C. Jones, CEO
Edmund M. Ackerman, President

Solution Tree Press
President and Publisher: Douglas M. Rife
Associate Publisher: Sarah Payne-Mills
Managing Production Editor: Kendra Slayton
Editorial Director: Todd Brakke
Art Director: Rian Anderson
Copy Chief: Jessi Finn
Production Editor: Paige Duke
Content Development Specialist: Amy Rubenstein
Acquisitions Editor: Sarah Jubar
Proofreader: Elisabeth Abrams
Text Designer: Kelsey Hoover
Cover Designer: Rian Anderson
Editorial Assistants: Charlotte Jones, Sarah Ludwig, and Elijah Oates

I dedicate this book to my two children, who teach me how to love better every day.

ACKNOWLEDGMENTS

Before I began writing this book, I had countless conversations with colleagues and friends, all of whom contributed greatly to the development of the ideas presented in the book. I want to acknowledge Prospect Sierra School for being the kind of place where I was able to develop curricula and deeply explore questions around equity, race, empathy, and inclusion. I want to acknowledge all my colleagues for their support and inspiration, and specifically Melody Esquer Gil, Jessica Walker, Jenna Ruby, and Cindy Pfost for contributing to the Peaceful Changemaker Curriculum. Thank you to Katherine Dinh, Abby Guinn, Nisa Frank, Britt Anderson, and Renee Thompson for their leadership and mentorship through this process. Thank you to Riti Dhesi and Bret Turner for agreeing to share their strategies and approaches to talking and teaching about race and racism in the classroom.

The work that Melissa Giraud and Andrew Grant-Thomas do at EmbraceRace (www.embracerace.org) has deeply influenced my ideas, and I recommend their website and webinars for any parent, caregiver, or educator interested in finding developmentally appropriate, antiracist ways to engage with children about race and racism. Thank you, Melissa and Andrew, for publishing my articles. I'm grateful for all our conversations.

Thank you to my editors, Sarah Jubar and Paige Duke, whose close reading of each draft of each chapter kept me on my toes!

Thank you to all my friends for listening and for agreeing to have a different version of the same conversation over and over again. Your questions and feedback were invaluable.

Thank you to my mother, Deborah Rogin, for modeling the beauty and strength of diving into the creative process and for always believing in me. Thank you to my sister, Isabelle Rogin, for helping me work out my ideas and for all her thoughtful suggestions. Thank you to my father, Michael Rogin, whose writings about race, racism, and White supremacy laid the foundation for my own thinking about these ideas. Thank you to David Leifer for asking thoughtful questions and offering your love and support.

Solution Tree Press would like to thank the following reviewers:

Liz Alfuente
Second-Grade Teacher
Ellicott City, Maryland

Amber Allen
First-Grade Teacher
Herriman Elementary
Herriman, Utah

Ian Landy
Principal
Powell River School District
Powell River, British Columbia, Canada

Eric Lindblad
English Teacher
Andover High School
Andover, Minnesota

David Pillar
Assistant Director
Hoosier Hills Career Center
Bloomington, Indiana

Sarah Svendsen
Kindergarten Teacher, Instructional Coach
Boca Raton, Florida

Kim Timmerman
Principal
Adel DeSoto Minburn Middle School
Adel, Iowa

Ringnolda Jofee' Tremain
PK3–8 Principal
Trinity Basin Preparatory
Fort Worth, Texas

Karly Ward
Principal
Rendezvous Elementary
Riverton, Wyoming

Neil Wrona
Social Studies Teacher and Technology Facilitator
Youth in Transition School
Baltimore, Maryland

Visit **go.SolutionTree.com/diversityandequity** to download the free reproducible in this book.

TABLE OF CONTENTS

ABOUT THE AUTHOR

Madeleine Rogin has taught children in grades K–4 since 2007. A change leader for Ashoka's Start Empathy Initiative and Changemaker Schools Network, she is an educator and dance teacher in the San Francisco Bay Area, California. Madeleine received U.S. recognition as the winner of the Great American Teach-Off in 2013 for developing the Peaceful Changemaker Curriculum as a way of teaching about Dr. Martin Luther King Jr. and social justice to children in grades K–4.

Madeleine is a member of the California Kindergarten Association, and in 2014, she won its Audrey Sanchez Teacher Enhancement Award. She delivers trainings for schools and families and presents throughout the United States on the topic of talking about race and racism with K–4 students. In the summer, she serves as a principal for a local public elementary school district.

Madeleine received her bachelor's degree in creative writing and urban education from Eugene Lang College, the undergraduate program at the New School for Social Research in New York City, a master's in dance with a focus on the African aesthetic in dance from the University of New Mexico, a teaching credential from St. Mary's College in Moraga, California, and a master's in educational leadership from the Bay Area Teacher Training Institute in Oakland, California.

To learn more about Madeleine's work, visit madeleinerogin.com or follow @madeleine_rogin on Twitter.

To book Madeleine Rogin for professional development, contact pd@SolutionTree.com.

PREFACE

Upon publication of this book, twenty-nine states have introduced bills or made other moves that aim to restrict schools' discussions of race, consequently limiting how teachers can talk about racism and sexism in schools (Strauss, 2021). A September 2020 presidential order blocked federal contracts to any diversity trainings that were *divisive* (Block, 2020). Diversity trainings could no longer discuss and examine implicit and explicit bias, White privilege, and systemic racism. In January 2021, the Labor Department suspended enforcement of this order (Guynn, 2021b). Additionally, in June 2021, federal lawmakers introduced legislation that would cut federal funding for schools that use lessons based on the 1619 Project, an ongoing *New York Times* project that aims to reframe American history by putting the consequences of slavery and the contributions of Black Americans at the center of the narrative (Silverstein, 2019).

In some cases, such as in Florida and Michigan, new rules prohibit schools from teaching anything from the 1619 Project (Silverstein, 2019). Other states, including Idaho and Oklahoma, have passed laws limiting the ways teachers can talk about race and racism in the classroom (Diaz, 2021). Though the efforts differ from state to state, these bans and restrictions share at least one stated common fear: that the teaching of racism as a structural, systemic problem, rather than a personal defect in individuals, will divide students in the classroom rather than unite them.

As a teacher and a parent, I am familiar with those fears. I used to believe that an honest exploration of differences would divide my students rather than unite them. Through years of practice, I've learned that the opposite is true. When given the facts about these differences—what they mean and don't mean, where they come from, and how they've been used in unfair ways to divide people and create hierarchies—students achieve a greater unity, one based in mutual understanding and respect (Derman-Sparks & Edwards, 2020). When young students receive ample time in the classroom to explore similarities, they discover what they have in common with people they think are very different from them (USC Rossier School of Education, 2021).

The fear that teaching about systemic racism will sow divisions among students, rather than create greater unity, is grounded in the false premise that these divisions and injustices don't exist already. Glossing over, minimizing, or ignoring racism in teaching history and social studies imply that issues of privilege, race, and racism haven't *already* influenced students' experiences as a determining factor in where they live and what kinds of resources they have. It presupposes that speaking openly and honestly about race and racism will create feelings of hostility, guilt, and mistrust, and that these feelings are not already present in classrooms all over the country.

The problem is that the story of the United States being post-racial and color blind, free of racism—except in the case of a few bad actors—does not ring true. A more honest approach that can lead to *greater unity and equity* in classrooms is one that accepts the fact of racism as a structural, systemic problem and teaches students what they need to know about race and racism to fight against racism at every turn.

It's important to know the ever-evolving rules in your state or province and what restrictions may be in place. No matter where you live—whether in the United States, Canada, or another part of the world—it's important to remember your teaching goals and be able to communicate them to anyone who would question your teaching practices. States and provinces that wish to ban teaching about race and racism in schools fear that this teaching will not only pit groups against each other, but also make certain students, namely White students, feel a sense of guilt about their race (Schwartz, 2021). The goal is not to shame students or to create hostility among groups. Teaching about racism does not create this hostility. To pinpoint and understand the genesis of this hostility in the United States, we can look as far back as the origins of Whiteness, a racial identity invented to justify slavery (Roediger, n.d.). The question is, *How do we talk about these difficult topics in a way that empowers all students, regardless of their race, to work against racism?*

The goal is greater understanding. Talking honestly about how the mistakes of the past continue to perpetuate racial inequities in institutions such as housing, health care, and education systems allows us to understand how to avoid repeating these mistakes. Learning to recognize biases and prevent them from forming enables us to create more respectful, empathetic bonds with one another across many areas of difference.

This book is grounded in my personal experience as a White kindergarten teacher and mother of biracial daughters who seeks to open conversations about race and racism in ways that create more unity in the classroom and address issues of injustice head on. This book is also supported by current theory on antibias and identity-safe practices and showing that these practices have documented, well-researched benefits for all students (Nguyen, 2021). Through storytelling, highlighting other educators' experiences, providing a historical and theoretical framework, and sharing research around best practices, I hope to demonstrate the power of breaking silences, not just for students in the classroom, but for all members of a school community.

INTRODUCTION

When I first began teaching about Martin Luther King Jr. to my kindergarten students, I didn't really talk about racism. There were several reasons for this. As a White teacher, I had limited firsthand experience with racism, and I had the privilege of choosing how and when to engage. Also, I didn't know what was developmentally appropriate to share with five- and six-year-olds, and I worried that this information would divide my class. At the same time, there were themes that Dr. King personified that I wanted to share with my students and children—themes of courage, social justice, and using nonviolent strategies to make change.

At first, I thought I could talk about these themes in a general sense, rather than connecting them to the actual struggle of the civil rights movement or ongoing efforts toward racial justice. Each year when it came time to celebrate Dr. King's birthday in my classroom, I talked in broad strokes about his dream of inclusivity. When reading books about his life, I rushed through or skipped over parts about segregation and his assassination. I recognized that students were not creating a deep understanding about the themes I cared about, but I didn't yet know how to change this.

Inevitably, a student would call out, "He was shot!" and classmates murmured on the playground and in the corners of the room about the violence surrounding Dr. King's death rather than talking about his life's work. A White student would point to a Black student and say something like, "She couldn't have sat at the front of the bus," and the Black student would look at me, waiting for my response. Because I didn't know how to proceed, and didn't know how to include all the voices in the room, I would stop the conversation.

I wasn't proud of this strategy. It didn't match with the kind of teacher I thought I was and with what I valued about teaching. I dreamed of creating respectful, inclusive classroom communities. I was committed to helping my students learn how to listen to one another, solve problems peacefully, and care deeply about one another and the larger community. They are the reasons I became an elementary school teacher in the first place.

My college self would not have recognized myself years later, sitting in front of a group of young students, closing a book before finishing it. My college classes hadn't prepared me for this moment; none of the books I'd read on teaching had described what I was feeling. Yet, I knew that keeping my students from talking about a subject because of my own discomfort with it was not good teaching.

In this introduction, I'll tell you a bit about my upbringing and explain how I came to understand my silence. As I confronted uncomfortable truths about myself, I learned to speak up about race in my personal life. I also recognized that teaching young students about race and racism is essential for cultivating respect and care in the elementary classroom. Of course, that is challenging work for many reasons, perhaps most of all because cultural attitudes about race and systemic racism inform our experience as teachers, both individually and collectively. Finally, I'll give you an overview of the book before we dive into part one.

How I Came to Understand My Silence

I grew up in Berkeley, California, in the 1980s, in a household where we talked openly about politics and how to create a more just and better world. I attended public schools in Berkeley, one of the first cities in the United States to desegregate their schools with two-way busing. All my elementary school classrooms were diverse. I was politically active as a teenager—I canvassed for local politicians and organized a teach-in at my high school during the Gulf War of 1990. My education hero was Paulo Freire (2000), author of *Pedagogy of the Oppressed*, who champions transformative education and giving people the skills and tools necessary to change their lives for the better. For all these reasons, I thought I would be good at leading conversations about racism with young students. Realizing that I was, in fact, unprepared to do so shook me.

I realized that speaking about racism is not a natural ability or a skill gained from one's environment; I had not yet built the competencies needed to engage in difficult conversations about race. How might my experience have been different if my kindergarten teacher or my parents had engaged in conversations with me about race and racism, and what it means to be White? Though most of my teachers were White, I don't remember any of them talking about their race, about the diversity in our classrooms, or how to understand and respect each other's differences. I did not have conversations with my family about race specifically, or what it meant to be White. When I discovered later that my father, a political science professor at UC Berkeley, devoted much of his work to issues around White supremacy and its inextricable ties to U.S. presidents, I marveled that the subject didn't come up in family conversations.

As I thought about my own discomfort around talking about race and racism with my students, I began to examine the conversations I had about race with my daughters, aged six and four at the time, who are biracial—I am White, and their father is Black Ghanaian. We had books in their bedroom library about skin color, including *The Skin You Live In* by Michael Tyler (2005), *All the Colors of the Earth* by Sheila Hamanaka (1999), and *The Colors of Us* by Karen Katz (2002). We had also intentionally bought dolls with brown skin and often talked about our different skin colors. (When they were very young, they had named my skin *vanilla*, their dad's skin *chocolate*, and their own skin *milk chocolate*.) However, I had not yet talked to them explicitly about racism.

One day, my older daughter brought home a picture book from school about Florence Mills, a Black singer in the 1920s, titled *Harlem's Little Blackbird* by Renée Watson (2012). As we read the book together, she stopped at a page that showed a group of White people holding signs that read "Whites Only." She looked up at me and said, "It was people with your skin who did this."

I froze, wanting to say something like, "No, no, my ancestors are Jewish, and they weren't even there!" But I knew I couldn't dismiss or deny the connections she was making about skin color, race, and privilege. I suddenly came face to face with my discomfort. I simultaneously realized why it is so hard for White people to have conversations about racism; feelings of guilt and discomfort can overwhelm and silence us. I eventually said something like, "Yes, and it was unjust and unfair."

She responded, "You're lucky because you could have gone into that theater."

By then I had taken enough deep breaths to be able to say, "But it wouldn't have been right to go in there or anywhere else where people with brown skin couldn't go."

As we read the rest of the book together, I paused at the photos of people who protested segregation, pointing out the array of skin colors of the protesters, and told her that's where many mothers with my skin color had been—standing up against the injustice of these laws.

That was the pivotal moment when I learned that it was impossible to teach my daughter—or my students—about who Dr. King was without also telling the ugly truth about racism. My daughter was asking me to help her make sense of this story. To support her development, I would have to engage in conversations about racism.

Why Teaching Young Students About Race and Racism Matters

As teachers, we tend to assume that students have sufficient foundational knowledge about race that allows them to grasp more complex topics around racism and societal injustices and engage in respectful conversations with their peers (Derman-Sparks & Edwards, 2020). Imagine if we made these same assumptions in our approach to teaching mathematics. What if we assumed that students had basic number sense and plowed ahead with algebra or geometry without first finding out what students already knew about numbers? We know better than that; we know the confusion that arises when we don't check for understanding, scaffold the learning, and provide appropriate supports. And yet, when it comes to the topic of race and racism, teachers often dive deep without doing any preassessments, with little or no sense of what students know or don't know. It's OK and appropriate to begin with the basics—including where skin color comes from and what race is and what it isn't—no matter the student's age.

In addition to offering students the foundational knowledge they'll need to navigate social justice issues, talking about race and racism creates a classroom culture where everyone works together to cultivate respect and mutual care. Educators Dorothy M. Steele and Becki Cohn-Vargas (2013) demonstrate that students thrive in school when they feel known and when their voices are valued. Only when students are allowed to take risks, challenge themselves, and learn to think critically about the world will the classroom become the safe space they need to thrive (Rogin, 2013). The social experience of the classroom plays a critical role in students' learning. According to Vygotsky's social development theory, knowledge is the product of the interaction between an individual and the environment, and understanding is social and cultural (Vygotsky, 1978). I wrote about this in an article called "How to Talk to Kindergarteners about Race" (Rogin, 2013):

> To this end, many schools have become devoted to . . . curriculum and schoolwide experiences that take into consideration the social and emotional lives of children—and how to help them navigate through conflicts, learn language to be inclusive with one another, and name and regulate difficult emotions that arise.
>
> Often this work on social and emotional health does not include explicit teaching about race, skin color differences, and racism.
>
> Too often we assume that, in our general teaching of how to be inclusive, our students will know how to communicate effectively across racial and ethnic differences.

Social-emotional learning is essential, but it doesn't go far enough to address racism. It turns out just teaching children to be *polite* or *kind* does not teach them the specific skills they need to communicate respectfully across differences (Derman-Sparks & Ramsey, 2011). For example, I used to notice a pattern of White students touching Black students' hair, which is a microaggression (Asare, 2020). I saw it in my classroom, learned it had happened to my daughter more than once, and heard about it from Black parents.

One of the skills in our social-emotional learning program is the personal space tool, teaching students to discern when and how to give their friends space. But this lesson on personal space did not stop the White students from touching the Black students' hair. At that point, I decided to teach students explicitly about different textures of hair. I explained that certain textures can be damaged from the oil on our hands. Together, we imagined how it feels to spend time on your hair only to have it messed up by someone else's fingers, and we brainstormed what they could do instead of touching. We also talked about how the behavior itself is disrespectful. Only then did my White students give Black students personal space around their hair. Helping my students learn how to respect one another required this *explicit teaching* about difference.

The goal of this teaching and learning, ultimately, is to disrupt patterns of bias, prejudice, and exclusion. It seeks to create classroom conversations and communities that are more cohesive, respectful, and inclusive by breaking silences that have led to ignorance and incompetence regarding race that would be unacceptable in reading, mathematics, or any of our other core academic subjects.

How Cultural Attitudes About Race and Systemic Racism Inform Experiences

Deep inequities across racial lines continue to exist in the United States, which has the greatest incarceration rate of any country in the world (M. Lee, 2015). In 2016, the United States confined more Black adults than were enslaved in 1850 (Carson, 2018). According to a Southern Poverty Law Center intelligence report, following the 2016 presidential election, "a wave of hate crimes and lesser hate incidents swept the country: 1,094 bias incidents in the first 34 days" (Potok, 2017).

In 2020, the United States experienced an uprising sparked by the killing of George Floyd by police in Minneapolis, and in response to many other unjust deaths of Black men and women, including Sandra Bland, Breonna Taylor, Elijah McClain, and Ahmaud Arbery, to name a few. According to data collected by *The New York Times*, in June 2020, anywhere from 15 million to 26 million people participated in Black Lives Matter demonstrations around the United States (Buchanan, Bui, & Patel, 2020). Protests spread to more than fifty countries around the world, with tens of thousands of people marching in places like London, France, and Australia, holding candlelight vigils in Iran, and attending protests against police brutality in Istanbul and Nairobi (Safi, 2020). These figures make these protests the largest movement in the country's history.

Because cultural attitudes about race and systemic racism continue to inform the experiences of U.S. citizens, and due to the fact that elementary students need explicit teaching about differences, their education must include learning around race and racism. Schools are faced with the challenge of grappling with how to best engage with students around these topics and include families in the conversation, as we attempt to create environments that promote inclusion as well as antibias and antiracist attitudes among students.

I believe that when we give students information about race and racism and the language to engage on these topics, they become more skillful at talking openly about differences and similarities, more confident in sharing their knowledge and ideas about social justice and racism, and less likely to become biased or to participate in prejudice or stereotyping. When families do this work at home, they reinforce and strengthen this learning. Yet families come to school with differing ideas about racial diversity and its value as a topic for family discussion. There is no common understanding or framework across schools and districts, which leaves educators to construct their own approach to talking to students about race or to avoid the discussion altogether.

What if teachers accepted the idea that young students need adequate preparation for a deep, meaningful understanding of racism and how to dismantle it? What if they identified the key, fundamental concepts students need to know first, similar to the way they teach basic number sense before teaching algebra or trigonometry? How would this lead to better outcomes? How would this create more unity and a sense of empathy around the topic? How could this reduce injustices and help to eradicate racism? This book seeks to answer those questions.

Book Overview

In this book, I explore with you how we can contribute to what professor and author Sheryll Cashin (2017) calls *cultural dexterity* or "an enhanced capacity for intimate connections with people outside one's own tribe, for seeing and accepting difference rather than demanding assimilation to an unspoken norm of whiteness" (p. 10).

I write from a specific perspective: that of a White teacher and mother of biracial children. The primary audience for this book is elementary school teachers and school leaders interested in breaking silences in their classrooms and school communities in order to disrupt bias and work against racism. This book is also written for any parent, caregiver, or other adult who spends time with young children and seeks greater equity and understanding by talking with them about race and racism. This book examines a specific experience of race in a specific context: a kindergarten classroom in an independent school in California.

This book tells the story of how I learned to talk about race and racism with my students and my daughters and invites you to consider the following lessons learned for yourself and adapt them for your classroom.

- Teachers can create conversations with elementary school students around race and racism.
- Kindergarten students can learn about changemakers and can acquire skills to become changemakers themselves. The same is true for diverse classrooms and for students of all ages.
- As a White teacher and mother, I can face my fear and discomfort talking about race and racism with children. Teachers can adopt strategies for facilitating dialogue, building understanding, and creating inclusive, empathetic conversations with students.
- Teachers have the power and responsibility to strengthen diverse communities and create more inclusive and equitable environments.

- Students can explore similarities and differences within their classroom community. Teachers can emphasize differences rather than being silent about them, they can teach about bias and prejudice, and they can cultivate a culture where differences are celebrated.

The book is divided into two parts. In part one, I explore four common reasons why teachers and parents or guardians stay silent about race and racism: (1) racial stress, (2) the belief that diverse environments are sufficient to teach students about race, (3) not knowing what to say about race, and (4) the desire to live in a post-racial world. Using research and anecdotal evidence, I'll make the case that these reasons are inadequate and that speaking up is a more effective strategy to creating equity and inclusion for all students. I include classroom activities to show what these strategies look like in practice. While some of these recommend books to read with students, you may benefit from consulting *There's More to the Story* (Cartledge, Yurick, & Telesman, 2022), a great resource for using literature to teach diversity and social-emotional learning to elementary students. I also share the approach of other elementary school teachers and draw from research I conducted with White elementary school parents about how often they talk with their children about race. Although I use examples of real-life people throughout the book, please note that names have been changed to protect individuals' privacy.

In chapter 1, we explore how becoming overwhelmed by racial stress causes people to retreat into silence. However, teachers can learn tools for managing racial stress and addressing racial conflict in the classroom. This chapter shows you how to lay foundational knowledge your students need to begin talking about race and provides sample classroom activities.

Chapter 2 examines a second reason White teachers cite for not talking about race: they believe that a diverse classroom environment will teach students how to be inclusive. While diversity has many documented benefits, it's not enough to counteract discrimination and stereotypes students encounter outside the classroom. Because stereotypes negatively impact student performance, teachers must go beyond diversity to create identity-safe classrooms where all students can thrive.

In chapter 3, I share my findings that many White parents or guardians don't introduce antiracist topics at home because they don't know what to say about race. My research on this topic led me to study the origins of Whiteness as well as its connection to White privilege and institutional racism. You'll access tools and sample lessons for helping students recognize the false stories culture tells about Whiteness and learn how to tell true stories about race.

Chapter 4 explores the reasons White parents wish for their children to live in a post-racial world. But because color-blind ideology fails to prevent microaggressions in the classroom, teachers must employ antibias education to help students celebrate all the ways we are alike and different and to address bias when it occurs. I share classroom activities you can use to integrate this learning with your students.

In part two, you'll read my story of recognizing my silence, creating the Peaceful Changemaker Curriculum, and talking to my students about race and racism.

Chapter 5 details my story of deciding to speak up. In 2010, I realized the way I'd been teaching Dr. Martin Luther King Jr.'s life and work did not include all voices, prevent students from singling each other out, or equip them to talk about standing up against injustice. In learning how to explicitly teach about race and racism, my team and I encountered four major challenges. I explain these challenges and share the action steps we took to address them.

In chapter 6, I outline the Peaceful Changemaker Curriculum my team and I developed. While students demonstrated huge growth, gaps in their learning indicated that the curriculum was still a work in progress.

Chapter 7 details my efforts to expand the Peaceful Changemaker Curriculum to include explicit teaching about race and racism. You'll discover the essential pieces of foundational knowledge I offered students around skin color, bias, and similarities and differences that paved the way for them to understand racism.

In chapter 8, we'll explore how to invite parents and caregivers to join the conversation about race and racism. Families have valuable insight, resources, and questions to contribute, and when teachers take a proactive rather than a reactive approach to family engagement, everyone benefits from the collaboration.

Chapter 9 examines five common roadblocks teachers face as they incorporate antiracist practices in the elementary classroom. You'll discover personal stories, actionable advice, and resources to address these roadblocks as you begin talking to young students about race.

The book ends with a glossary of common terms and a robust appendix section packed with resources to support your learning and efforts to share your learning with your students. Appendix A offers answers to frequently asked questions from parents, caregivers, and colleagues; appendix B contains a list of children's books that address skin color, race, hair, and related issues; and appendix C recommends books for adults on race and racism.

Moments of Connection

Young students are full of questions and bursting with ideas about how to solve problems and keep things *fair*. One of the most rewarding aspects of being an elementary school teacher or a parent of a young child is observing aha moments—those times when a young child learns something new, makes a connection, or works through a personal learning struggle. These moments of connection can be even more meaningful when they lead to a stronger, more unified classroom community, and when they disrupt patterns of exclusion or injustice.

The issues the book explores—bias, prejudice, exclusive versus inclusive behavior, race as a social construct and lived experience, and the dangers of racism as it relates to young students in school communities—are, as my students put it, "big and affect everybody." My hope is that this book will offer concrete strategies for engaging with young students around these important topics, strengthen relationships across differences, and help to eradicate racism.

PART ONE

Reasons Some Choose Silence and Reasons for Breaking It

In the end, we will remember not the words of our enemies, but the silence of our friends.

—Dr. Martin Luther King Jr.

In part one, we'll examine four common reasons for silence: (1) racial stress, (2) the belief that diverse environments are sufficient to teach students about race, (3) not knowing what to say about race, and (4) the desire for a post-racial world. We'll look at each of these reasons in detail; explore what research and anecdotal evidence tell us about why these reasons are inadequate for staying silent about race; and discover why speaking up is a more effective strategy for achieving equity, inclusion, and belonging for all students. Along the way, I share relevant keywords, topics, and classroom activities I found helpful on my journey to speaking up about race with elementary students.

CHAPTER 1

RACIAL STRESS

The day my eldest daughter and I read *Harlem's Little Blackbird* by Renée Watson (2012) together, she voiced that people with *my* skin color had oppressed people who looked like *her*. In that moment, I grappled with some big feelings. I sensed that whatever I said in response was important, possibly more important than any other difficult topic we would ever talk about. I felt like I had to get it right. I knew that saying the wrong thing could be extremely detrimental to her and to our relationship. I also felt the need to defend myself, even though she wasn't talking about me—she was talking about a system of injustice and oppression carried out by White people against Black people. For a moment, I was paralyzed. My heart sped up. I felt a buzzing in my temples and the sensation that I had lost all my words. I looked down at the picture of singer Florence Mills, who had been invited to perform in New York City when she was a child. She stood with her family as an angry White man held out his hand to block her family from going into the theater. Behind him, a group of White people held a "Whites Only" sign.

What made this conversation more difficult than others? Why did I suddenly feel like I was trying to paddle upstream in a rowboat with no oars? I was struck by the desire to say, "I wasn't there! It wasn't me!" I worried that saying the wrong thing would reveal something bad about me. Since then, I've learned through reading the work of Robin DiAngelo (2012) and Ali Michael and Eleonora Bartoli (2014) that this desire to be seen as someone who is not racist was interfering with my ability to engage fully in the conversation.

In this chapter, we'll start by examining why people often retreat into silence in response to racial tension and how that silence is a response to racial stress. I'll discuss how teachers can learn to manage racial stress so they can respond to racial conflict by speaking up instead of staying silent. We'll explore how to lay foundational knowledge your students need to engage in conversations about race, consider two sample classroom activities, and discover how to set the tone for dialogue about race.

Understand Silence as a Response to Racial Stress

Psychologist Howard Stevenson (2014) calls experiences like the one I had with my daughter moments of racial stress. *Racial stress* is the overwhelming feeling of dealing with racial encounters, which affects people of all races and impairs an individual's thoughts, behaviors, emotions, and relationships. In Stevenson's (2014) view, the desire to remain silent when faced with racial stress is an avoidance coping strategy that arises out of a deep fear of engagement.

Research suggests that White parents and guardians, in particular, respond to racial stress by adopting color-blind attitudes and teaching their children to do the same. Researchers Jamie Abaied and Sylvia Perry (2021) studied a sample of 165 White parents following the deadly Charleston church shooting in 2015, finding that White parents tend to avoid conversations about race and racism with their children. Even when these conversations increased in 2020, following George Floyd's death, White parents tended to adopt a color-blind approach when talking to their children about race, or waited to have these conversations until their children were older (Abaied & Perry, 2021). In a 2016 study of 107 White mothers of children ages four to seven, 81 percent reported it was important to have conversations about race, while only 62 percent reported having them. Of these, 70 percent displayed a color-blind approach (Vittrup, 2016). Researchers Ali Michael and Eleonora Bartoli (2014) write about why White families perpetuate color blindness:

> Most of the white families [opt] to socialize their children by telling them not to be racist, not to talk about race, not to use the word "black," and not to notice racial differences. They [want] their children to believe that all people are the same and that racism is bad.

The idea that by not talking about or seeing race White parents will raise "natural" nonracists, and conversely, that bringing up race somehow contributes to racism, is a common theme among White parents and educators, as well as children

(Bronson & Merryman, 2009; DiAngelo, 2012; Michael & Bartoli, 2014; Tatum, 1992, 1994, 2017; Vittrup, 2016; Wise, 2012). In contrast, research on racial stress and racial literacy suggests that parents of color tend to have more frequent conversations about race. Howard Stevenson's (2014) research focuses on how Black parents help their children navigate discrimination and prepare them for anticipated discrimination by engaging in racial socialization, or a teaching about race that develops children's cognitive abilities to understand the meaning of racial discrimination.

In the classroom, it's this type of engaged approach to racial socialization that provides students the skills and tools they need to combat racism and form meaningful connections across cultures. Avoidance may reduce the current level of stress, *but it does not lead to greater competence over time* because the ability to engage is blocked. Howard Stevenson (2014) writes:

> Without admitting to and managing our fears, we remain unprepared for racial conversations, encounters, or conflicts. Trying to improve race relations and combat racial stereotypes without addressing the stress that is generated by these endeavors is like trying to solve algebraic equations without understanding multiplication or learning to drive a car without lessons. (p. 3)

What is the impact of this discrepancy between how often White parents bring up race as compared to parents of color? What happens when some students come to school well versed in issues of racism, and with a sense of their own racial identity, and others do not?

One possible outcome is that when racial incidents occur in schools, the impact is not experienced equally among families of different racial backgrounds, and students miss out on opportunities for greater growth and understanding.

I've experienced this outcome firsthand. In the spring of 2016, during the presidential election cycle, unbeknownst to me and my colleagues, a kindergarten student at my school announced during lunch that there was going to be a war at the White House between White and Black. Following that statement, another student said they should "play the war game" after they were done eating. What ensued was a game of tag that involved some students chasing two Black students around the yard. The chasing group was mixed, some White students, some Asian students, but the targeted students were Black. The teachers on the yard thought the kindergarteners were playing their usual game of tag, until the two girls who were being chased ran to one of the teachers and asked for help.

The spring of 2016 was a particularly tense time, and it didn't surprise me that students were acting out in their play some of what they were hearing in the media or during conversations between adults at home. Young children often act out social issues in their play to make sense of them. Modern interpretations of developmental theory tell us that play is the key method that children use to understand their world (Jones & Reynolds, 2011). It came out later that the student who talked about a war had meant for it to literally be a race, which made me wonder if he hadn't heard words like *presidential race* and *White House* and—picking up on a general sense of tension and conflict, especially around race—conflated terms.

In the aftermath of the event, families of color took a more proactive approach to addressing the issue than White families did. In response, the administration sent home an email describing how our teaching team had handled the incident: we held a community circle and addressed the dangers of targeted play and exclusion, reinforced the idea of allyship and safe play, and offered resources for parents to continue the discussion at home. The parents of the girls who had been chased, along with other parents of color, requested that the school schedule a mandatory meeting for *all* students' parents and guardians to talk about what had happened and make sure it didn't happen again. In contrast, several of the White parents did not feel the need for any further action. In fact, some said they had been too busy to read the email and felt assured that the school had handled it well.

The parents of the Black children involved in the incident were concerned that the White parents would not talk about the incident with their children at home and that the children who chased their kids would not understand how dangerous and problematic is this type of play. They feared that these families would retreat into a silence that would cause further harm to their children.

Start the Conversation

When racial incidents happen at your school, what can teachers do to facilitate conversations instead of staying silent? How can you support student understanding and growth, and how can you involve families in this learning in a way that will deepen understanding for all involved? Teachers should provide guidance for students to support them in moving through conflicts, and they should reach out to families in order to communicate about the incident and what the school will do to resolve it.

Provide Guidance for Students

Howard Stevenson (2014) suggests that teachers should teach students how to "read, recast, and resolve racially stressful social interactions" (p. 4) in order to support them in becoming racially literate. Let's look at each step in more detail.

1. **Read the conflict:** Gather information from the students involved in the incident in order to understand what happened and consider each person's perspective.
   - *Allow students to share their version of the story*—Have everyone involved tell you what happened, as you would with any conflict or problem between students. Ask general, information-gathering questions, such as, "Tell me about what happened," rather than questions that tend to put students on the defensive, such as, "Why did you say that?" or "Why would you do that?"
2. **Recast:** Provide strategies to help reduce the stress.
   - *Provide students tools to manage the stress*—Help your students recast, or locate the stress in their bodies, and give them strategies to help reduce the stress. Stevenson (2014) offers a racial recasting skill that both children and adults can use: *calculate*, *locate*, *communicate*, *breathe*, and *exhale*. Teach your students how to calculate, on a number scale from 1 to 10, the stress they are feeling, locate where it is in their bodies, communicate what they are feeling, breathe, and exhale. Teach this strategy *before* any incidents occur to let your students know that these things will happen, and there are strategies they can use to manage them.
3. **Resolve the conflict:** Support the students and families involved in the event in resolving the conflict together.
   - *Schedule a class meeting or facilitate a conversation*—Decide if the incident warrants a class meeting or a facilitated conversation between the involved students. Emphasize the impact of the conflict, which could be hurt feelings due to teasing or exclusion, rather than the intent of the person who displayed the exclusionary behavior. This could sound like, "What we want to pay attention to is what happened as a result, and how we can

make sure this doesn't happen again." By placing value on the impact or outcome, you are communicating that even "good" people can make mistakes. This allows teachers to reinforce the importance of working together as a community to reduce the number of mistakes we make.

» *Try role-playing*—Students in grades K–2 respond well to puppet plays and other role-playing activities, where the focus and attention shift briefly away from them. This allows them to act as problem solvers, to "help" the puppets work through their problems, and to practice scripts they can then use with each other when necessary. Choose two puppets that are similar. Have the student act out a scenario where they make fun of another puppet for being different or not like them. Ask your students to name what's happening (read the conflict), making sure to name bias and prejudice if the students don't, and ask them what the puppets should do to resolve the conflict. Young students will often talk directly to the puppets in earnest, even if afterward they say that they knew "those were just puppets."

Reach Out to Families

Let families know right away when something happens, and be transparent about how you dealt with it in the classroom. If the incident involves a clear victim, as the one on the playground did, reach out separately to those families to gather their feedback about what they hope will happen in resolving the incident.

Looking back, I wish we had held a mandatory meeting after the playground incident. Bringing everyone together to address what happened would have been a powerful opportunity to read, recast, and resolve. As I discovered later in my own research, parents of color at my school had reason to be concerned that White parents weren't necessarily going to have conversations about what happened on the playground at home.

Work Through Racial Stress

Building competency for working through racial stress is different from teaching math or reading. When students or adults make mistakes or say something insensitive, the impact can potentially be harmful; that's much less likely in conversations about academics. So, how can teachers proceed with care and sensitivity toward classroom and family communities? And what are some helpful ways to manage and work through racial stress when it arises?

As we look at three strategies in the following sections, remember that maintaining a goal-centered approach is helpful. Teachers' top priority should be to achieve greater competency, shared understanding, and more unified communities. With these goals in mind, what are some specific ways teachers can build competency for themselves and support students and families in doing the same?

The Growth Mindset and Cultural Competence

First, teachers can adopt a growth mindset to supporting students in becoming culturally competent. Carol Dweck (2017), psychology professor at Stanford and leading researcher on motivation and mindsets, is well known for her work on growth mindset. Put simply, a *growth mindset* is the "belief that your basic qualities are things you can cultivate through your efforts" (Dweck, 2017, p. 7). By contrast, students with *fixed mindsets* think their intelligence and abilities are inherent traits, "carved in stone" (Dweck, 2017, p. 7). In the classroom, fixed mindset comments sound like, "I just know that because I'm good at math," or "I'll never be able to draw because I'm a bad artist."

To support students in moving from fixed mindset to growth mindset, teachers should demonstrate that while students' outcomes and achievement matter, they're more concerned with students' making the effort to learn and engage in the process of continual growth. According to growth mindset theory, rather than giving general praise by saying things like, "Good job!" or "That was really smart!" teachers should praise students' efforts and engage in conversations about the thinking behind the work (Dweck, 2017). This could sound like, "I can tell you spent a lot of time on that," or "I'm curious to know about your approach to this problem."

Many schools and classrooms have adopted the growth mindset approach to teaching academics. When it comes to areas of cultural competence, though, teachers tend to slip back into a belief that basic qualities are fixed traits (Lee, 2015). Because we have a collective experience of being uncomfortable about racism, it's easy to forget that the discomfort and challenges are invitations to growth and development.

Embracing the growth mindset in our work around identity, inclusion, and cultural competence has the potential to improve our experience because, just like in academic areas, we will begin to pay attention to development and effort over performance and results. This has powerful ramifications for the classroom and for including families in the learning. As one parent told me, "It helps to know my mistakes don't mean I'm a bad person." Consider the following examples of how to shift your language to reflect growth mindset rather than fixed mindset.

- "I'm uncomfortable—I must be learning" versus "I'm not good at this"
- "Mistakes are inevitable—I'll try a different way next time" versus "I didn't get it right the first time"
- "This requires regular practice" versus "I've already had this conversation"

Shifting from fixed mindset to growth mindset takes time and practice, but the benefits are well worth the effort.

The Pit and Learning Challenges

In addition to encouraging students to adopt a growth mindset, teachers can help them work through racial stress by fostering what James Nottingham calls *learning challenges*. James Nottingham (2017), cofounder and director of Challenging Learning, strives to encourage "learners to investigate contradictions and uncertainties so that they might more deeply understand what it is they are thinking about" (p. 1).

One strategy Nottingham (2017) uses is called *the pit*. Students are in the pit when they have a set of unresolved, contradictory ideas about something they are trying to understand—when learning *feels hard*. To help students build resilience and stay engaged, teachers encourage students to be in the pit, where they are having multiple ideas at once and thinking deeply about them. The goal is not to get the right answer but to pursue deeper understanding and engagement. To get students into the pit, Nottingham (2017) recommends creating learning challenges—activities and discussions that create a state of cognitive conflict, in order to make the learning more challenging and thought-provoking.

Students have a keen sense of justice and are often adamant that everything should be fair. This leads to plenty of opportunities for learning challenge conversations with them. Consider the following examples.

- Is it fair that every president of the United States, except for one, has been a White man?
- Is it fair that most students in the United States learn about Columbus but don't learn about the many Indigenous tribes that lived on North American land long before Columbus arrived?

- Is it fair that some students have access to their own personal computers or to online learning while others do not?

The list could go on and on. Young students have conversations about fairness with each other constantly and are often eager to participate in teacher-facilitated discussions. Nottingham (2017) writes:

> The Learning Challenge relies on high quality dialogue. At its best, dialogue is one of the best vehicles for learning how to think, how to be reasonable, how to make moral decisions and how to understand another person's point of view. It is supremely flexible, instructional, collaborative, and rigorous. Done well, dialogue is one of the best ways for participants to learn good habits of thinking. (p. 9)

Importantly, as with any dialogue, learning challenges only work when students have a basic, shared understanding of the concepts they are discussing. While all learning challenges are necessarily complex, those that arise around race and racism can elicit stressful reactions that block dialogue and end discussions. To support students in staying engaged, teachers can provide clear guidelines and parameters to these discussions, such as community agreements, definitions of commonly used terms, and strategies to manage stress.

Racial Recasting

Managing racial stress isn't just for students; teachers need to actively practice the skills to be ready to respond to situations that arise in the classroom and to model the behaviors for their students. Misinformed statements and difficult questions from young children can bring about racial stress for teachers or can make you feel as if you've lost your words.

Howard Stevenson's (2014) racial recasting strategy of calculate, locate, communicate, breathe, and exhale is an excellent tool to lean on in such moments. What might it look like to apply it to your competency building as a teacher?

- *Calculate* the level of stress you are feeling.
- *Locate* it in your body.
- *Communicate* about this stress to yourself. Recognize any self-talk you are doing during the experience, and work toward shifting from negative ("I can't do this") to positive ("I can work through this") self-talk.

- *Breathe* deeply for the span of three full breaths, putting your full attention on each inhale. This can help you calm your senses and ground yourself in the present moment.
- *Exhale* through another round of three full breaths, focusing on the exhale. Practice letting go of the places in your body where you are holding stress.

It may also help to have scripts at the ready. For example, "What you just said is important, and we need to talk about it more. I care about this topic, and I want to answer you with the best information I can find. Let me do some research and get back to you." When I say this to my five- and six-year-old students, they often nod gravely, appreciative of the fact that an adult is taking their ideas and questions seriously.

With guidance and support from their teachers, students as young as five and six can apply these strategies as well.

- *Calculate:* Invite students to use their fingers to show their level of discomfort or stress on a scale of 1–10.
- *Locate:* Ask students to rest a hand on the place in their body where they are feeling this stress.
- *Communicate:* Instruct students to talk about this stress with you. Together, work to shift from negative ("I can't do this") to positive ("I can work through this") self-talk.
- *Breathe and Exhale:* Ask students to close their eyes, take three deep breaths, and focus completely on their breath; first the inhale and then the exhale. Tell students that the act of focusing on their breath helps to calm their bodies and reset their attention and focus.

Looking back at that moment with my daughter on the couch reading *Harlem's Little Blackbird*, I realize I had some strategies at the ready: I took a deep breath, I gave myself time, I engaged in positive self-talk ("You can do this even though it's hard"). The look on my daughter's face, like she was truly confused and connecting dots all at the same time, helped me stay focused on the goal of the conversation. It was my job to let her know that I am her ally and her support, and as her White mother, I will always fight against injustice and racism.

Build Students' Foundational Knowledge

When we teach a student to read, we start with the alphabet. We teach letter recognition, letter sounds, and basic prereading skills, such as rhyming, hearing sounds in words, and breaking words into discrete parts. We continually check for understanding and reteach when necessary, and we practice in some way, usually every day, in the classroom. Therefore, when we teach students to become competent in talking about race and racism, we can start by laying a strong foundation of understanding. The following list includes some foundational concepts you can explore with young students.

- What race is and what it isn't
- How race has operated and continues to operate in the United States and other countries
- Our own internalized biases or misinformed ideas
- What we can do to create more equitable experiences in our classrooms
- Definitions of common terms students will encounter in conversations about race (see the glossary, page 145)

As we practice talking about these definitions and ideas with students, we also work on how to communicate across differences with respect. As teachers and students build their capacity to manage racial stress, they'll gain the tools for staying engaged instead of retreating into silence. To be able to do this work with students, teachers must already be doing the work for themselves. If you're just beginning your personal work around breaking silence, investigating your personal bias, and adopting antiracist practices, you can explore helpful resources in this book's glossary (page 145) and appendices A (page 147), B (page 157), and C (page 161). There you'll find definitions of common terms, frequently asked questions, and books for students and adults about race and racism.

Now let's look at two sample activities you could incorporate into your classroom to lay foundational knowledge about race.

Classroom Activity

WHEN YOU THINK YOU'RE DONE, YOU'VE JUST BEGUN

Race is a difficult and complicated concept. It's different from skin color and ethnicity. It is a social construct, and yet is has real meaning and power. Students, no matter their age, need to know that skin color is not the same thing as race. They need to be taught that there's no way to know by looking at someone what their race is and that there's real danger in making assumptions about people based on what you *think* you know by looking at them.

Create anchor charts for these ideas, as you discuss them, just as you would to ground a writing lesson. In my classroom, we have an anchor chart at the Writing Center that reads, "When You Think You're Done, You've Only Just Begun." The chart lists specific things students can add to their writing when they think they are finished: they can add details to the picture, add a character's emotions, or check for capitalization and punctuation. Create a similar chart customized to your conversations about race, and use it during classroom conversations. The steps will vary depending on the age you are working with but could include the following.

- Challenge your assumptions.
- Learn more.
- Ask questions.
- Challenge your assumptions again.

Classroom Activity

COUNTRIES TELL STORIES ABOUT THEMSELVES

Julius Lester's (2005) *Let's Talk About Race* is a great resource for helping students begin to define race. His definition is, in part, that race is a story that countries make up about themselves. Lester (2005) writes, "Just as I am a story, and you are a story, and countries tell stories about themselves, race is a story, too" (p. 16). We all have a race as part of the stories we tell about ourselves, which is helpful for

White students, who may be struggling to locate themselves racially and to begin to understand that this story of race in our country is about them, too (page 43). Lester (2005) goes on to say that some stories are true, and some are not true, and the story that one race is better than another is a story that is not true.

After sharing this idea with your class, have students think of one thing about themselves their classmates wouldn't know by looking at them. You may choose for students to write, draw, or share about their trait. This activity helps to reinforce the idea that we can't truly know anything about anyone by looking.

Set the Tone

Once you've clarified your definitions and thought of different ways to share them with students, it's important to set consistent community agreements and expectations. Your classroom should have shared ground rules for how everyone will engage with conversations about race. I've had success with developing a class charter, surrounding students with positive associations, discussing skin color, and communicating classroom goals with families. The following sections look at each of these in more detail.

Develop a Class Charter

One way of establishing shared guidelines is to develop a *class charter*, a social-emotional learning tool developed at the Yale Center for Emotional Intelligence (Charter for Compassion, n.d.). In the first week of school, the class decides how they want to feel at school and what actions will bring these feelings out. When you have serious discussions, refer to the charter and hold each other accountable for making sure everyone is still feeling the way the students have chosen (for example, happy, excited, safe, and curious). Talk about what students can do when they have other feelings, which will naturally happen, but not ones students want to intentionally cause (for example, mad, sad, furious, or embarrassed). Communicate that it's OK for students to take a brain break in the cool-down area of the classroom, draw a picture about their feelings, communicate verbally with the friend that made them upset, or get help from an adult.

These protocols give a predictable structure to help support students when something goes wrong in their play, in their learning, or in the middle of a conversation about any topic, and especially topics that can elicit strong feelings.

Surround Students With Positive Associations

It's important to inundate students with positive associations and conversations about race, and particularly about Blackness, before they talk about racism or any type of societal injustice. Forming positive associations supports students in gaining appreciation for the topic and fostering curiosity and excitement rather than fear and shame. It's easy for students to experience fear and shame during conversations about race if they don't have a foundation of understanding, appreciation for differences, and protocols for how to communicate as a community.

I'm not advocating for a superficial celebration of multiculturalism. Teachers should engage in deep reflection to ensure that the classroom environment and the curriculum represent multiple identities and center voices that have been traditionally excluded from educational institutions. As researchers Dorothy M. Steele and Becki Cohn-Vargas (2013) write:

> When teachers limit their diversity efforts to pictures on the wall, an occasional assembly, or the celebrations of food and cultures in a way that does not truly engage students in learning about one another, their students miss opportunities to feel valued and to gain respect and curiosity not only about their different histories, languages, cultures, and perspectives but also about their own identities. (p. 67)

Chapter 5 discusses this topic in greater detail.

Discuss Skin Color

Before beginning any difficult conversation about race or racism, make sure you have spent a good amount of time discussing skin color. Reinforcing the idea that everyone has a skin color works against the idea that White is the norm. It's also essential to engage in activities that decrease bias against Blackness.

In early conversations about skin color with your students, emphasize the facts about how we get our skin color (the sun, where our ancestors came from, and melanin). Emphasize that each of us has skin color, that there's no such thing as good or bad colors, or better or worse colors, and that the only way to know anything about a person is to get to know who they are, to know their story.

For a deep dive on this topic, see chapter 3.

Communicate Classroom Goals With Families

Engaging families in the teaching, and learning from what they tell you, are another important part of beginning the work. Teachers should let parents and caregivers know what their values are and why they are initiating learning around race and racism.

First, identify what you want your students to be able to know and do by the end of the unit, just as you would with any unit of study. For example, "The goal in my classroom is to lay a foundation of understanding so that my students will be able to have more productive, less biased, respectful connections with one another and a deeper appreciation for what it takes to be a changemaker, or to work toward positive social changes in our society."

Once you are clear on your goals, communicate them to families and ask them what their child knows already about this topic. When I first asked the question, I was surprised to receive a bag of books from one family. These books (*The Story of Martin Luther King Jr.* by Johnny Ray Moore [2015], *We March* by Shane W. Evans [2016], and *A Sweet Smell of Roses* by Angela Johnson [2007]) turned out to be the cornerstone of many of my lessons.

Establishing trust in the beginning of the year goes a long way toward working through any missteps or issues that may arise later. This should be a continual process, and one grounded in respect, especially for families who have been traditionally excluded from decision making in educational institutions.

Chapter 8 discusses parent engagement in more detail.

Learn the Power of Yet

In *Sesame Street*'s (2014b) "Power of Yet," a cast of puppets expresses its frustration at not being able to achieve certain tasks. With the help of singer, songwriter, actress, and producer Janelle Monáe, the puppets learn a new way to think about these *failures*. Rather than saying, "I can't do this," the puppets learn to say, "I can't do this *yet*." My kindergarten students have adopted this language, and I often hear them correcting each other. When someone says, "I can't do it!" another student will call out, "You mean you can't do it *yet*."

As we think about our challenges, discomforts, and doubts about talking about race and racism, and the confusion that can arise among students, it's helpful to remember that we are often in the pit. The pit is not a bad place to be. Being in the pit just means we haven't fully understood or grasped the ideas *yet*. This is not the same thing as condoning biased or ignorant statements in other adults or in our students. It is a way to stay on the "what you said" rather than "what you are." Luckily, young students present us with plenty of possibilities to focus on the "what you said," if we are willing to listen.

CHAPTER 2

DIVERSE ENVIRONMENTS

One morning, I stood on a neighborhood playground, watching my daughters play on the swings. Another White parent stood next to me, watching her son play on the monkey bars. As often happens, we started talking about our kids. Out of the blue, this parent told me, "You know, my son never says, 'That's my African American friend' about his friends at school who are African American. He never refers to people by their skin color. He just says, 'That's my friend.' Isn't that great?"

I was taken aback, wondering why she had decided to share that with me and unsure how to respond. I immediately thought of my older daughter the day before, sitting on a bench with another biracial child. They had their shirtsleeves pulled up and were holding their arms close together. "We match!" my daughter said, looking over at me, smiling. There were few Black children on the playground at the time, and I could tell she felt happy, safer, knowing that she had a "match." While the other parent noticed that her son didn't see race, I heard that my daughter valued being seen as a minority in a White majority environment.

In chapter 1, we saw that White parents often remain silent as a response to racial stress. In this chapter, we'll examine another reason White teachers give for not talking about race: they believe diversity itself will teach students to be inclusive. We'll explore this claim by looking at documented benefits of diversity, how bias and discrimination inhibit these benefits, and the effect of stereotypes on student performance. I'll also share how creating identity safety in the classroom poses an antidote to stereotype threat.

Benefits of Diversity

Parents who rely solely on diversity as a teaching tool hope their children will learn about tolerance and respect from diverse friendships rather than through conversations about race. As one White parent put it, "I don't want to mess with their friendships by putting my baggage on it." Another White parent told me, "There's something pure about the friendships they are making. I don't want to spoil that." Journalists Po Bronson and Ashley Merryman (2009) developed the Diverse Environment Theory, which describes this desire to let diversity do the teaching rather than engage with students about diversity. In their book *NurtureShock*, Bronson and Merryman (2009) encapsulate the belief in this way: "If you raise a child with a fair amount of exposure to people of other races and cultures, the environment becomes the message" (p. 55). The idea is that *just* being part of a diverse community, rather than having explicit conversations about diversity, will teach students the skills they need to decrease bias and develop respectful bonds with one another (Natkin, 2013).

This idea raises essential questions: What kinds of messages do students get from diverse environments? Are these environments capable of creating the conditions that allow all students to thrive, without explicit instruction around this diversity and what it means? Is what's going on between students when they are interacting across race, or forming cross-racial friendships, *pure*, or untainted by any societal messages or biases?

Racially, economically, and linguistically diverse learning environments have many well-documented benefits. Consider the following positive elements supported by research.

- Diverse school environments promote tolerance, interrupt bias, improve academic achievement, and promote civic participation (EdBrief, 2019).
- Students have the opportunity to build cross-racial friendships, practice empathy, and work on social-emotional skills (Kamenetz, 2016).
- Researchers Gary Orfield, John Kucsera, and Genevieve Siegel-Hawley (2012), of UCLA's Civil Rights Project, have conducted extensive research on whether desegregation leads to an improvement in children's racial attitudes. Orfield and colleagues (2012) find that desegregated schools lead to benefits for all students, including

"prejudice reduction, heightened civic engagement, more complex thinking and better learning outcomes in general" (p. 7).

- Katherine Phillips (2014), of the Columbia Business School, focuses on the cognitive benefits of encountering racial and ethnic differences. Her research shows that "bringing together different viewpoints and experiences makes everyone think harder and provides better evidence for their opinions" (Phillips, as cited in Kamenetz, 2016).

Constructing diverse and inclusive environments is an indispensable part of socializing kids to be tolerant and inclusive. But does it go far enough to interrupt discrimination, uproot bias, and equip students to engage in social justice? According to scholars who contributed to the 2007 amicus brief to the Supreme Court supporting school desegregation in Louisville, Kentucky, and Seattle, Washington, the benefits of desegregation are not guaranteed (Parents Involved in Community Schools v. Seattle School District No. 1, 2007). The brief states, "Such positive outcomes become stronger when optimal intergroup conditions are established in the school environment. Racially diverse schools can be structured in ways that make positive outcomes more likely to occur" (Learning for Justice, n.d.b). Without guidance through this experience, students can continue to form prejudiced or stereotypical ideas about racial and ethnic differences, among others.

The Smog

Award-winning educational leader and best-selling author Beverly Daniel Tatum (2017) calls prejudices and stereotypes part of the *smog* of racism that penetrates all our institutions, including our schools. She describes this smog as consisting of messages about race perpetuated in media, including children's books, movies, video games, songs, TV shows, news programs, racial inequities in a student's neighborhood, school, or wider community, what a student's parents have said—or not said—about race, as well as any messages the student received from peers or teachers (Tatum, 2017). When teachers and other school professionals don't actively work to clear the air of prejudices and stereotypes, this smog obscures students' ability to understand and celebrate differences within their community. The conclusions they reach about why people are different and what these differences mean aren't unprejudiced but often misinformed.

In her book *Caste,* Pulitzer Prize winner Isabel Wilkerson (2020) further illuminates how the media perpetuates smog-filled messages about Blackness:

> Little more than one in five African-Americans, 22 percent, are poor, and they make up just over a quarter of poor people in America, at 27 percent. But a 2017 study by Travis Dixon at the University of Illinois found that African Americans account for 59 percent of the poor people depicted in the news. (p. 234)

Examples of the Smog

I'll share two examples with you to illustrate how the concept of smog can manifest in the classroom. One afternoon, I asked my kindergarten students to think about where they noticed different races, outside of our classroom and school community. I was curious to learn what they were noticing in their neighborhoods, how they were seeing race. One of my White students raised his hand and said, "I see Black people who are homeless." The fact that he primarily associated Blackness with poverty disturbed me. This might have made sense if he was developing a foundational understanding of how systemic racism has led to current inequities, but, as I'd learned from talking to his parents, my classroom was the first place he was having these conversations, so his understanding was limited, and smog filled.

Doubt filled my mind, and my heart raced. How had his comment made the Black students in the room feel? After taking some breaths, I said, "You and I need to talk more about this so we can understand what you're seeing and noticing. It's also true that there are many, many Black people who are not homeless, but who may not live in your neighborhood, but who do live in neighborhoods you haven't been in."

That night, I did some research and came to school the next day prepared to talk to my student in more detail. Research shows that while Black people constituted less than 10 percent of Berkeley's general population in 2017, they represented 50 percent of the homeless population (City of Berkeley, 2017).

"What you're noticing is an unfair pattern of a greater number of Black people without homes than White people in our area," I told him. "That has to do with what's called systemic racism, or unfair rules that have made it more difficult for people of color to have the same opportunities as White people in our country." This conversation with my student allowed us to discuss how racist policies result in inequities across race. Without this, my young student could have concluded that such inequities across race are a result of personal choice, defects, or shortcomings, rather than a reflection of systemic racism.

This theme, of associating Blackness with homelessness, came up in several interviews I conducted with parents. As one parent explained, "We talk about [race] when the situation arises, when we see a homeless person or panhandler." This parent's choice to only talk about race in the context of poverty could likely reinforce stereotypes about Blackness, resulting in comments like the one my student made about only seeing Blackness in homelessness.

Another time, a student shared about a recent trip to visit family in Egypt and shared photos that included women wearing hijab. Another student came up to me afterward and said, "I know why those women were wearing scarves on their heads. It's because their hair is dirty."

I said, "That's actually not why they cover their hair. Let's learn about this." And we did, by reading about hair-covering traditions in multiple cultures. We learned that covering hair is a sign of respect. The student shared this learning with other students in the class. Had I not addressed this student's misinformed idea about hair, I wonder how his idea that *those* people have *dirty* hair would translate into further prejudice and bias.

The problem with waiting to engage with White children until they see race is that White children who live in primarily White homogeneous environments can tend to only see race when they travel to more heterogeneous, or urban, or mixed communities, and start to form misinformed ideas about race (Winkler, 2012). Additionally, when White children associate Blackness with poverty, they are expressing biased ideas about Blackness.

Smog and Stereotype Threat

In addition to promoting bias and discrimination, smog can impact student performance. *Stereotype threat* shows up in class when students experience the cognitive burden of perceiving they have to work against a stereotype about their social identity. Developed by psychologist Claude M. Steele, stereotype threat describes the powerful hold of identity on a person's psyche, "a hold so strong that the person stereotyped is adversely affected even by being afraid to confirm a negative stereotype" (as cited in Cohn-Vargas, 2012).

In his book *Whistling Vivaldi,* Steele (2011) shares the story of Brent Staples as a young Black psychology graduate student at the University of Chicago, walking through Chicago's Hyde Park neighborhood:

> I became an expert in the language of fear. Couples locked arms or reached for each other's hand when they saw me. Some crossed

> to the other side of the street. . . . I tried to be innocuous but didn't know how. . . . I began to avoid people. I turned out of my way into side streets to spare them the sense that they were being stalked. . . . Out of nervousness I began to whistle . . . popular tunes from the Beatles and Vivaldi's *Four Seasons*. The tension drained from people's bodies when they heard me. (p. 6)

By whistling classical music, Staples was trying to dispel the bad stereotype that Black men are prone to violence. "The example demonstrates the psychological toll borne by all African American men in a society that fears them" (Cohn-Vargas, 2012).

In the context of the classroom, the toll of stereotypes can often manifest in underperformance. "Individuals underperform in tasks for which negative stereotypes about aspects of their collective or social identities—be it race, age, gender, or nationality—exist" (Zhang, 2014). Steele (2011) experimented with stereotype threat by recruiting men and women at the University of Michigan to take advanced mathematics and English exams. Women did worse than the men on the mathematics tests, where they reported feeling more stigmatization or stereotype threat, but performed equally well on the English tests, where they did not report feeling stigmatization, even though no one was actively invoking the stereotype at the time the women took the test. When Steele repeated the experiment and presented the test as not showing any gender differences, the women and men performed equally well.

Steele and his colleagues repeated these experiments with Black students, invoking different stereotype threats, and the results were the same, proving the effect of stigma pressure can be generalized to other groups. Continued research shows that students seem to have the psychological development needed to experience stereotype threat by age five or six (Régner, Steele, & Huguet, 2014). Teachers should understand that students don't just perform worse on tasks when a stereotype is invoked (for example, "women aren't good at mathematics") but also when a stereotype isn't actively addressed and negated; as the name suggests, the *threat* of the stereotype is enough to create adverse effects.

Reducing Stereotype Threat

Steele's (2011) work reminds teachers that it's not enough to make sure we aren't exhibiting stereotypes. As historian, activist, and author Ibram X. Kendi (2019) writes, "There is no neutrality in the racism struggle. The opposite of 'racist' isn't 'not racist.' It is 'anti-racist'" (p. 9). For us as teachers, being *neutral* would mean assuming there are no stereotypes present if we are not explicitly presenting them to our students. An antiracist approach, on the other hand, recognizes that inequities don't exist merely because of individual attitudes and beliefs but are also created by systems and power.

What practices can teachers adopt to interrupt stereotypes? Many teachers begin this work through inclusion by representing diverse identities in the pictures on their walls, voices in their curriculum, and books in their classroom library. Consider the following additional suggestions for reducing stereotype threat in the classroom.

- **Check your own stereotypes:** Make sure that you critically examine your beliefs about your students' social identities. Learn about diverse identities. Read Zaretta Hammond's (2015b) *Culturally Responsive Teaching and the Brain* for suggestions on how to recognize and combat your own stereotypes. Reflect on classroom procedures, such as the way you construct seating charts and how you call on students. Whose voices are most present in classroom discussions? Invite a trusted colleague to observe your teaching practice and reflect back to you whom you've called on or permitted to speak the most. Who are the leaders in the classroom, and how can this role be shared equitably?
- **Have students develop self-affirmations:** Give your students time throughout the year to write about or draw what's important to them. Provide an opportunity for students to share why this is important to them. Younger students can respond to prompts such as, "I care about . . ." while older students can write paragraphs about two to three of their most important values. Studies show that such self-affirmations, by bringing forward a sense of self-competency and worth, can improve academic performance (Steele, 2011).
- **Emphasize a growth mindset:** Throughout the year, show your students images of the brain making new neural connections as it learns new things. Emphasize that the brain is like a muscle in that it grows stronger with hard work and effort (Dweck, 2017). By stressing the expandability of intelligence, you are working against the stereotype that some people are just good at school while others aren't.

Additionally, Steele suggests "saturating the environment with cues that show interest in diversity and highlighting role models with minority identities who have achieved success" (as cited in Kramer, 2016).

Combating Stereotype Threat With Identity Safety

Hoping to find solutions to stereotype threat, Claude Steele—along with his wife, Dorothy Steele, and colleagues—developed the concept of identity safety and tested it repeatedly in the classroom. Becki Cohn-Vargas (2012) describes the results:

> They found that when students were in an environment where they felt valued, where their identities and ideas were considered to be a resource, where they could develop positive relationships and it was assumed they would achieve, their performance and liking of school improved. In addition, the negative consequences of stereotyping and stereotype threat were reduced.

Dorothy Steele and Becki Cohn-Vargas's (2013) work emerged out of the research on stereotype threat. In *Identity Safe Classrooms*, Steele and Cohn-Vargas (2013) offer a valuable, practical resource for elementary and middle school teachers interested in implementing activities and an approach to teaching that will reduce stereotypes and lead to greater success for all students. Their research, involving eighty-four diverse elementary school classrooms, identified effective practices that are linked to improved student outcomes in standardized tests and improved attitudes about school. They call these practices *identity-safe practices* because they provide potential antidotes to stereotype threat. Steele and Cohn-Vargas (2013) write, "We discovered that with careful attention to providing challenging instruction and by facilitating positive social dynamics in the classroom, students of all backgrounds came to feel accepted, included, and expected to be successful" (p. 6).

There are four key elements to identity-safe practice: (1) child-centered teaching, (2) diversity as a resource for teaching, (3) classroom relationships, and (4) caring classrooms. Table 2.1 includes suggested practices for each element. This is an extremely brief and abbreviated list. The book devotes entire chapters to each practice.

Putting Identity-Safe Practices Into Action

I've seen firsthand the power of bringing identity-safe practices into the classroom. After thinking about whose voices were most present in my classroom discussions, I realized that my White, male students seemed to talk the most. As a

TABLE 2.1: Four Key Elements to Identity-Safe Practice

Identity Safety Element	Suggested Practice
Child-centered teaching: Put students' perspectives at the center of classroom practices.	To help students focus on social understanding and to build a sense of collaboration and cooperation into daily practice, introduce social goals in addition to academic ones. This could sound like, "For this partner mathematics activity, our social goal is that we take turns and share the materials. What are some ways we can take turns fairly?" Give your students time to reflect on social goals after lessons, just as they reflect on the academic goals.
Diversity as a resource for teaching: Celebrate all types of differences, which stands in direct contrast to a color-blind approach to teaching.	Invite each student's family to share something about them with the class. Give families a range of choices in how and what they present, with the awareness that some parents and caregivers have more time during the day than others, so things like classroom visits may not end up being equitable. The student could bring in photos, a special book, or an object that represents the family culture. Before beginning these sharings, come up with silent hand signals with your students that allow them to connect with one another. For example, if they hear something that resembles their family, they could put a finger on their nose, and when they hear something that's different from them, they could pat their head. This allows all students to make connections with one another, as well as reinforcing the idea that we all have similarities and differences with one another.
Classroom relationships: Develop positive relationships, both between the teacher and the students and among students as the foundation of identity-safe classrooms.	Introduce the daily practice of giving shout-outs at class meetings, end-of-day circles, or whenever the class is gathered as a community. Shout-outs are a time for students to appreciate one another, and their teachers, for specific acts of kindness or support. This practice fosters positive relationships between teacher and student and among students. Pay attention to any emerging patterns, such as certain students receiving shout-outs more than others, and discuss this problem with the class. Ask your students how it might feel to not get a shout-out, and how good it feels to get one. Compliment students who give inclusive shout-outs, such as, "I want to appreciate the whole classroom and everyone in it!"

continued →

Identity Safety Element	Suggested Practice
Caring classrooms: Engage rather than control students, providing emotional and physical comfort and paying attention to prosocial development (such as respect, empathy, and listening).	Devote a corner of the classroom to be a problem-solving area, a place where students can draw and write about problems they are having with friends. Hold a weekly meeting to solve these problems together, as a class. Students can act out the problem and come up with solutions, or use puppets to act it out. Certain rules must apply: students cannot write individual names, and no one is required to share.

Source: Adapted from Steele & Cohn-Vargas, 2013.

result, I decided to change the way I called on students. I put their names on popsicle sticks, put the sticks in a cup, and told my class that I would pull names during class discussions, rather than asking them to raise their hands. I also let them know that they didn't have to speak, that they could pass if they weren't ready to share. Pulling sticks did allow for more voices to be present, but the students I most wanted to hear from, the ones who had been the quietest, who also happened to be Black, passed every time.

I decided to check in with these students one-on-one throughout the week, using conversation techniques designed to build empathy, rather than put students on the defensive, such as, "I've noticed . . ." and following up with, "What's up?" I knew these techniques would communicate to students that I wanted to understand their concern or perspective rather than control or change their behavior (Greene, 2014). I learned that my assumptions, that the students weren't paying attention or were bored, were wrong. One said of a boy who talked often in class, "He always has the answer" and told me that his classmate's tendency to shout out the answer made him not want to try. Another student had a lot to say but didn't want to speak in front of the whole class.

In response to this feedback, I decided to make more shifts to the way we talked as a class. I began talking about my own values to my students. I told them that I cared about everyone's voice being included in a discussion much more than I cared about whether anyone got the right answer. I asked my students to help me think of ways we could hear from everyone. As a class, we decided to give more wait time for people to think. I waited to call on students, and they waited to speak, for the most part. We decided that calling out the answer was like "opening someone else's present" and everybody should be able to "open their own present."

I also began doing more turn and talks, or partner talks, and I introduced non-verbal leadership roles, such as coming to the front of the room to help me set up learning boards. The student who didn't feel comfortable sharing in front of the class helped me develop hand signals he could use to let me know when he was ready to share, without the discomfort of having everyone's eyes on him. These shifts led to greater equity in our class discussions.

Classroom Activity

CLEARING THE SMOG

What should teachers do to clear up the smog as they begin talking about race with students? What are the critical conversations and experiences that will help to interrupt bias and prejudice? Building understanding of how fairness, opportunity, and generational wealth impact current income disparities is particularly important. In the elementary classroom, teachers can integrate these ideas into mathematics and social studies lessons. Consider the following classroom activities for clearing the smog.

- During a unit on money, demonstrate how much easier it is for money to increase and multiply when you start with some, rather than none. Allow students to use puppets to create a puppet or Stuffy Town to simulate how this works in real life.
  - Set prices for things they need to purchase, such as food and housing. Distribute play money unevenly among the students. Let your students know that the stuffed animals with money inherited it from their families while others didn't. Make sure that each student has the opportunity to have stuffed animals with more money, and ones with less. It won't take long for the students to realize how much easier it is to get their stuffy's basic needs met when they start out with money, especially if jobs are scarce in Stuffy Town.
  - To help students understand the impact of systemic racism on income disparity, make some unfair rules for Stuffy Town, such as the cat or zebra stuffed animals can't purchase homes or get help from a bank to purchase homes. Ask students, "Why isn't this fair? What can we do to change it?" They will most likely suggest, "Get

continued →

rid of those unfair rules!" Help them notice that these stuffed animals, the ones that have been excluded from purchasing homes or borrowing money, are the ones that didn't have money to start out with. So, even if the rules change, they still must find a way to get the necessary funds. Ask them, "How have those unfair rules made it harder for them to have the same things as the other stuffed animals?" These experiences are powerful because they allow students to gain a sense of empathy (young students care deeply about stuffed animals and fairness) and a new understanding of the problem.

- Make sure that each area of instruction includes Black people as sources of knowledge. Here are a few examples to get you started.
    - Research scientist Patricia Bath invented a technique used to remove cataracts (Changing the Face of Medicine, n.d.).
    - Shirley Jackson is responsible for monumental telecommunications research (Schaffer, 2017).
    - The research of mathematician Gladys West laid the foundation for the creation of the Global Positioning System (Mohdin, 2020).
    - Biochemist Marie M. Daly opened up new understandings of how food and diet can affect the heart (Wright, 2021).
    - Alvin Ailey's dance, *Revelations*, is the most widely seen modern dance work in the world (Kennedy Center, n.d.).
    - Kerry James Marshall is a contemporary artist whose mission is to make the presence of Black people and Black culture in the art world undeniable (Stamberg, 2017).
- Teach your students the facts about differences in the classroom—including skin color differences, hair differences, and language differences—always emphasizing the idea that you can't tell everything about someone by looking at them. Look for places in your teaching that may be heavily influenced by smog. If you teach in a racially homogenous environment, this requires explicit instruction about differences that may not be represented in your student population but that all students need to understand in order to clear the smog. After the experience correcting the student's misconception about hijab, I began teaching the facts behind hijab and other hair coverings each year before

showing any images or opening any discussions that could include this difference.

- Make sure your physical environment is full of images and books representing historically marginalized groups doing everyday things as well as amazing things. For help in diversifying your classroom library, check out www.leeandlow.com and the post "Building a Diverse, Anti-Bias Library for Young Children: A Masterpost" on the blog Equity in Early Childhood (Madison, 2015).
- Help students in grades 3–5 understand how the messages they receive from media can be biased by teaching them to critically analyze what they consume. For this activity, instruct students to watch a local or national news hour, keep track of how many stories about poverty and crime are about people of color, and then conduct research to record actual statistics around poverty and crime. According to Wilkerson (2020), crimes involving Black suspects and White victims make up 42 percent of crimes reported on television, even though these crimes make up a minority (10 percent) of crimes committed.

A Way Through the Smog

Diverse environments offer powerful lessons to students. But because students are subjected to smog in media and institutions, diversity doesn't go far enough to inoculate kids against discrimination. Teachers must explicitly address stereotypes in the classroom by creating identity safety. In the next chapter, we'll explore the kinds of learning we hope to cultivate for students and the role White privilege plays in our understanding of race.

CHAPTER 3

NOT KNOWING WHAT TO SAY ABOUT RACE

In chapter 1 (page 13), we saw that socializing students about race, rather than remaining silent on the topic, equips students to engage with topics of social justice. I've witnessed this firsthand along my journey of learning to talk about race. Over the years, I noticed that my White students know less about race than their peers of color; I've heard White students make assumptions about students of color, a pattern that bothered me so much it led me to completely change my curriculum and approach to the topic (which I discuss in part two, page 75). My classroom is sometimes the first place these students learn about melanin and get the true story about where skin color comes from.

I started to wonder about how students were learning about race from their families and caregivers. I'd never asked any White parents how they approached this topic at home. If they did bring it up, what did they say? And if they didn't, why not? Were their conversations very different from the conversations parents of color were having? Were they having any conversations about race at all? As part of my graduate studies in educational leadership, I decided to conduct a research project at my school, an independent school in the Bay Area, about how often parents talked about race with their children in early elementary grades. In 2018, I surveyed seventy-eight parents of first- and second-grade students and sat down for in-depth interviews with ten of these parents. At the time, our school comprised 45 percent students of color and 55 percent White students. The racial demographics of my sample study mirrored the racial demographics of the school. I chose to interview White parents to learn more about their reactive stance toward race (as opposed to the proactive stance among parents of color), a pattern I observed in the survey data. I was interested to find out the following.

- How, when, and why this topic came up at home
- Whether the topic was initiated by the child (or children) or by the adults
- How competent adults felt they were in leading this discussion
- How much they thought their race influenced their comfort level
- The overall value they placed on the topic, as compared to other subjects they discussed with their children

Most White parents I interviewed expressed varying levels of anxiety and uncertainty about what to say about race and how and when to talk about it. They expressed a variety of reasons for not engaging with the subject, such as waiting for their child to be older or hoping the school would broach the topic. Parents expressed the fear that they didn't have the *right* words, an often-recurring theme that contributed to a general sense of incompetency. Comments included the following.

- "I could definitely use more tools."
- "I would like to discuss it more with my child but don't always know which elements of the discussion are most appropriate for her age."
- "I am White and feel guilty about the advantages my race provides, and I'm also fearful about acting or speaking 'incorrectly' around issues of diversity, especially when speaking about it with people of color."

As I reflected on these interviews, I realized I'd been wrong to assume that White parents weren't talking about race at all. The parents I interviewed did talk about it, but most often in response to a question from their child or following an incident or learning at school, rather than as a planned conversation with specific goals in mind. As one parent said, "I don't think we address it proactively at home." And it wasn't just that parents didn't know what to say in moments of racial stress. They didn't know what to say about race in general. What are the ramifications of this for our everyday work with students and families in our elementary school programs?

In this chapter, I'll share how answering those questions led me to examine Whiteness. We'll examine the origins of Whiteness, what it means to have White privilege, what it has to do with institutional racism, the stories we tell about Whiteness, and how to tell accurate stories about race. I've included classroom activities along the way that you can use to communicate what you're learning with students.

The Origins of Whiteness

I understood the struggle I encountered during the parent interviews. In my efforts to talk about race and racism with my students, I kept running into the discomfort of naming my own race in front of my class. The first time I told my class that I was White, I felt like I'd said something wrong or too revealing. I was worried one of my students would ask me what it meant to be White because I had no idea how to respond. I could have talked about my father's Jewish background, or my mother's time in Catholic schools as a teenager, but at the time I didn't yet understand how that related to being White.

If I was going to understand my own racial identity and figure out how to teach in a way that wouldn't ignore Whiteness or perpetuate patterns of silence, I needed to understand more about where Whiteness comes from. I first turned to researcher, counselor, and teacher Shelly Tochluk's (2010) book, *Witnessing Whiteness,* which helped me understand my discomfort in speaking about a racial identity that's been made invisible in our culture, how it originated, and its inextricable ties to racism. Whiteness, as a racial category, developed over time, and in the United States is inextricably linked to ideas such as humanity, freedom, access, and self-determination.

Tochluk (2010) attempts to uncover this history by examining the moment in time when ideas around a White race were constructed. She writes that while terms such as *white* and *black* were used when Europeans first encountered West Africans, they were mostly used to describe skin color differences related to environmental factors, such as exposure to the sun. The idea of a White race was constructed later in colonial history to justify a permanent status of enslavement for Black Africans (Tochluk, 2010). A narrative was created about racial differences, affording white skin with "God-given" innate qualities of goodness, and black skin with the opposite. American historian Howard Zinn writes, "[Enslaved Africans] were impressed again and again with the idea of their own inferiority to 'know their place,' to see blackness as a sign of subordination" (Zinn & Arnove, 2015, p. 35).

The ideology of White supremacy was made up to justify enslaving Africans. This narrative of racial difference became a determining factor in forming democracy in the United States. As journalist Ta-Nehisi Coates (2017) points out:

> It was slavery that gifted much of the South with a working class that lived outside of all protections and could be driven, beaten, and traded into generational perpetuity. Profits pulled from these workers, repression of the normal angst of labor . . . formed a foundation of democratic equality among a people who came to see skin color and hair as defining features. (p. 66)

Despite the abolition of slavery and the many advances made toward racial equity since the nineteenth century, White supremacist mindsets endure. If we hope to continue to build a more just and equitable society, we must acknowledge the ways racism informs our lives, and we must share that information with students through developmentally appropriate practices.

White Privilege Defined

How does White supremacy inform twenty-first century life in the United States? That narrative of racial difference persists in the form of *White privilege*, which is a set of benefits granted to those who, by race, resemble the people who dominate the powerful positions in our institutions. One of the primary privileges is having greater access to power and resources (Kendall, 2013). To understand what White privilege is, it's helpful to think about what White privilege is not. Educator and Learning for Justice senior writer Cory Collins (2018) writes:

> [White privilege] is *not* the suggestion that white people have never struggled. Many white people do not enjoy the privileges that come with relative affluence, such as food security. Many do not experience the privileges that come with access, such as nearby hospitals. And white privilege is *not* the assumption that everything a white person has accomplished is unearned; most white people who have reached a high level of success worked extremely hard to get there. Instead, white privilege should be viewed as a built-in advantage, separate from one's level of income or effort. (p. 39)

Collins helps us link historical ideas around race and skin color privilege to present racial inequities. The fact that white skin was afforded built-in advantages at this country's founding has ramifications for today, as it meant that those without white skin did not have access to the same systems and structures.

Peggy McIntosh's (1988) seminal paper "White Privilege and Male Privilege: A Personal Account of Coming to See Correspondences Through Work in Women's

Studies" discusses White privilege as a system of unearned advantages. McIntosh (1988) writes:

> I have come to see white privilege as an invisible package of unearned assets that I can count on cashing in each day, but about which I was "meant" to remain oblivious. White privilege is like an invisible weightless knapsack of special provisions, maps, passports, codebooks, visas, clothes, tools, and blank checks. (p. 2)

McIntosh (1988) lists many examples of these privileges: White children in the United States learn from curricular materials that testify to the existence of their race and teach that people of their race made their national civilization what it is today. White people don't have to worry about being targeted because of race when pulled over by the police. White people have an easier time buying posters, postcards, picture books, greeting cards, dolls, toys, and children's magazines featuring people of the same race (McIntosh, 1988).

Since 1988, there have been many advances in the effort to ensure representation of races other than White. There has been an increase in racial diversity on corporate boards, such as S&P 500 companies, though the rate of change has not equaled that of gender diversity in this area (Barney, 2020). There are more children's books that feature characters of color, though books with White main characters and animals continue to be published at a more frequent rate (Huyck & Dahlen, 2019).

As adults, how do we explain this to young children? Can they understand how certain people benefit from unfair systems that were set up before they were born, that continue to influence the kinds of opportunities available to everyone in our society? Spend some time on an elementary school playground, and you'll see that young students are hyper aware of issues related to power and privilege. You might hear students debating why some people try to be "everyone else's boss" by exhibiting too much power over their peers, or why some people think they have the privilege of having more of their share of a classroom treat, more time with a favorite piece of playground equipment, or a longer time on the swings.

Although it is challenging to engage students on this topic, it is certainly possible. When Bret Turner taught first grade in Oakland, California, he dedicated himself to finding a way to talk about these ideas with his six- and seven-year-old students so that they could be equipped with the vocabulary, tools, and confidence to continue engaging with difficult subjects as their understanding grew more nuanced (personal communication, June 2020). For example, when Turner taught about money, he facilitated a discussion about representation, pointing out that all the faces featured on the coins and bills belong to White men. When students learned how to skip count by twos, they practiced counting U.S. senators and kept track of how many senators are people of color, female, or both.

Along the way, the class had numerous conversations about whether the lack of representation of people of color was fair or not fair. Turner says about these conversations, "My first graders had learned a lot of general rules around kindness and what it means to stand up for themselves and others. The way I included ideas around racism and White privilege is the idea that certain hurts hurt deeper. And, that it's not always about being 'nice.' It's about working to make things more fair" (B. Turner, personal communication, June 2020). He talked about this on a societal level by reflecting on the injustice and hurt of not being included in important places, such as in government, based on the color of your skin. Asking students the question, "What is the problem of excluding based on race or skin color?" is one way into a conversation about privilege and power.

Institutional Racism Defined

Discussions of White privilege must acknowledge racism at both the individual level and the collective level. In *How to Be an Antiracist,* Kendi (2019) makes an important distinction between individual acts of racism, racist policies, and institutional racism (also called systemic racism). *Institutional racism* refers to racist structures or processes perpetuated by groups with power, such as governments, businesses, or schools (Collins, 2018). Institutional racism is about the racial inequities that emerge from racist policies (Kendi, 2019).

One approach is to emphasize that racism isn't a past problem that society has overcome; it is an ongoing, systemic problem that we must keep trying to solve. Teaching racism in the past tense might sound like: "Today we are going to learn about some unfair rules that used to apply to people of color in our country and how those rules were changed in order to make things fair and more equal." By contrast, present-day teaching about racism could sound like: "Today we are going to begin learning about an unfair system of rules, patterns, and biases that was invented long ago, at the founding of our country, and continues to make things less fair and equal for people of color."

It's all too common for celebrations of the achievements of the civil rights movement to leave out the other parts of the story: continued struggles, backlashes, and current examples of racial inequities. As Bryan Stevenson (2014), founder of the Equal Justice Initiative and author of *Just Mercy,* writes, "It seems to me that we've been quick to celebrate the achievements of the civil rights movement and slow to recognize the damage done in that era" (p. 300).

Throughout history, racism did not disappear when laws changed; instead, as Wilkerson (2020) writes, racism mutated to "adjust to the updated needs of the software system" (p. 68), the *software system* being the structure and ranking of racial hierarchy. It is the "granting or withholding of respect, status, honor, attention, privileges, resources, benefit of the doubt and human kindness to someone on the basis of their perceived rank or standing in the hierarchy" (Wilkerson, 2020, p. 70). One way White supremacy functions is to attempt to maintain this racial hierarchy at all costs.

What are other ways teachers can emphasize institutional racism? Consider the following suggestions.

- When you talk about racism with your students, stay in the present tense. Celebrate the achievements and gains of the civil rights movement while also being honest about the ongoing struggles.
- Emphasize that it is especially important to avoid making assumptions about people of color because of the history of prejudice and racism directed toward them. This could sound like, "While it's not OK to make assumptions about anyone, we have to be vigilant about not making assumptions about people of color, and that has to do with racism. If we don't work at it, we may find that we are stereotyping people. Stereotypes are dangerous because they can cause us to exclude, hurt, or treat people unfairly. One way to be an antiracist is to be on the lookout for any stereotypes of people of color."
- When you talk with students about systems of privilege and power, be explicit about the racism inherent within these systems. This could sound like, "One reason there's only been one Black president is because of racism. For example, for many, many years Black people were not allowed to vote, and there are still obstacles today that make it difficult for Black people to vote." Consider teaching about the following.
    - » Students in grades 3–5 can learn about the Voting Rights Act of 1965, which outlawed the discriminatory voting practices adopted in many southern states after the Civil War. The Supreme Court invalidated key parts of the Voting Rights Act in 2013 (Liptak, 2013), which allowed states to return to some of

their previous practices, including redistricting, or the process of dividing an area into new political divisions without first seeking permission from the federal government to ensure that these plans didn't discriminate on the basis of race.

» Students in grades K–2 can learn about some of the obstacles that made it difficult for people to vote, including literacy tests as a prerequisite to voting.

------ *Classroom Activity for Upper Elementary Students* ------

STUDYING POLICE RESPONSES

On January 6, 2021, the day that Congress met to certify the results of the 2020 presidential election, thousands of predominantly White protestors gathered at a rally. A mob from within this group made its way to the Capitol, overwhelmed police, broke through barricades, smashed windows, and occupied offices. Some sprayed officers with chemical agents and looted sizable objects. Homemade bombs were discovered at two locations, and a man was arrested for possessing firearms and materials to make Molotov cocktails. Several people died. Though members of Congress had warned the chief of police about the riot four days before it happened, the police seemed unprepared (Dewan, MacFarquhar, Kanno-Youngs, & Watkins, 2021; Haberman, 2021).

The police response to the riot on January 6 was very different from police response to Black Lives Matter activists in the summer of 2020. In Oregon, peaceful protestors were gassed and beaten, especially when they neared federal buildings. On June 1, 2020, Black Lives Matter protestors in Washington, D.C., were met with rows of masked National Guard troops.

For this activity, allow students to compare and contrast images of police responses to the 2021 attack on the Capitol (as well as images of people roaming the Capitol building) and the 2020 Black Lives Matter protests. Use this article in *The Guardian* to compare and contrast photos: "MAGA v BLM: How Police Handled the Capitol Mob and George Floyd Activists – In Pictures" (Borger, 2021).

Ask your students why they think the rioters at the U.S. Capitol on January 6 were dealt with more peacefully than protestors at Black Lives Matter protests in the summer of 2020. After viewing these images, ask students to respond to the quote from Attica Scott, a state representative from Kentucky: "You can be arrested for walking while Black, but you can be white and riot and basically get away with it" (as cited in Dewan et al., 2021).

Ask your students: "What roles do you think White privilege and White supremacy can play in police response?"

End the lesson by discussing ways to act, including writing letters to local government officials, learning more, and speaking out against these kinds of hypocrisies.

The False Story of Whiteness

Underlying silence is often the false assumption that there is no collective White racial identity. White antiracist activist Tim Wise (2012) writes:

> While we are quite used to referring to . . . people of color in terms of their group identity, we insist on referring to ourselves individually, almost as if to suggest that we lacked a racial identity, or that if we possess one, it contains no relevance to our lives. (p. 20)

For those considered White, the often-unspoken assumption that White is *normal* or not a race was part of the process of becoming American. Due to evolving immigration policies, what it meant to be White changed over time, depending on which immigrants were deemed most desirable (Zinn & Arnove, 2015). The Immigration Act of 1924 limited the number of immigrants allowed entry into the United States from certain hemispheres, including Southern and Eastern Europe, and completely excluded immigrants from Asia, while increasing the number of more "desirable" immigrants from Britain and Western Europe. Wilkerson (2020) writes that, at that time, "these groups [Poles, Jews, Greeks, Italians] were not always extended the protections accorded to unassailably 'white' people" (p. 123). Writer James Baldwin (2010) puts it this way: "The price of the ticket was to cease being Irish, cease being Greek, cease being Russian, cease being whatever you had been before and to become 'White'" (p. 156).

Part of "becoming White" meant agreeing to a deep, cultural silence about White racial identity, because to truly see Whiteness, you must also see the oppression of non-Whites, and to acknowledge how the two are inextricably connected. The film *I Am Not Your Negro* (Peck, 2016), based on Baldwin's unpublished manuscript about the assassinations of Medgar Evers, Malcolm X, and Martin Luther King Jr., uncovers how Whiteness in the United States is intertwined with a collective desire for innocence and a forgetting or refusing to accept, atone, or reckon with crimes of our past.

I'd like to share a personal example of a time I encountered the false story of Whiteness. The following excerpt is from an article published by *InCultureParent* about my struggle to talk to my daughter about police officer Darren Wilson's acquittal for the killing of Michael Brown in Ferguson, Missouri, in 2014:

> I wondered, sitting at a quiet restaurant facing my nine-year-old daughter, how much Wilson's description of Brown influenced the jury's decision—more than the witnesses who testified that Brown had his hands in the air and was trying to surrender when he was shot. How much did Darren Wilson's bestial, demon-like portrait of the man he killed contribute to his acquittal? . . .
>
> In an attempt to prove his innocence despite these facts [that he had a weapon as well as non-lethal options including a baton, flashlight, and mace], Wilson reaches back in our history . . . of viewing whiteness as innocent and vulnerable and blackness as scary and overpowering. In this narrative, even white police officers with guns who won't carry tasers because they are "uncomfortable," are somehow more innocent and human than the unarmed black men they pursue. . . . The jury accepts this narrative and finds him innocent. (Rogin, n.d.)

Teachers must interrupt false narratives of Whiteness, such as this, if we are committed to disrupting racist thoughts and actions in the next generation of students and encouraging them to dismantle racist systems that continue to harm people of color.

Classroom Activity

TALKING ABOUT RACE

Julius Lester (2005) begins his children's book, *Let's Talk About Race*, with a question: "How does your story begin?" (p. 3). He goes on to write about his own story, what he likes to do, what his favorite foods and colors are, and so on. When he introduces race, he writes that race is a part of all our stories. Just as each person is a story, so countries tell stories about themselves, and race is a story, too (Lester, 2005). Using Lester's (2005) book as a starting point, complete the following steps to talk with students about race.

1. To begin the conversation about White supremacy and institutional racism, read this story to your class, or reread it if you've already read it in a different context (such as defining terms). This time, the goals are more about getting at the roots of White supremacy and institutional racism.
2. Let your class know that you are going to talk about the story of how race began in North America. Start with White supremacy. Tell your students that Whiteness was developed as a racial category to justify horrible acts against people who weren't White. Make clear that this is not a conversation about students in the class or any individual people in the room. Put this in simple terms for your young students by connecting the story of Whiteness to Lester's (2005) message that "Some stories are true. Some are not. Those who say, 'my race is better than your race' are telling a story that is not true" (p. 16). By beginning there, you are beginning where the story about race began in North America.
3. Ask your students to think about why people might want to say their race is better than another's. Generate a list, titled "False Stories." Add any ideas students may offer in response to the question about why someone would want to say their race is better than anyone else. You may suggest "The false story of White supremacy," and tell your students that this is a very dangerous false story that people tell because of its devastating impact on communities and generations of people of color.
4. When the list is complete, tell your students you are going to generate a new list, one that is titled "True Stories," and have them think of things that are true about our differences with one another. Read or reread books like Katie Kissinger's (2014) *All the Colors We Are*, Michael Tyler's (2005) *The Skin You Live In*, and Bobbi Jane Kates's (1992) *We're Different, We're the Same*.

Guide students to consider:

» What you can and can't tell about someone from their skin color

» What skin is and what skin isn't

» How we are alike and different

continued →

5. Remind your students, after you have created the list, that stories matter, and it is our job, as antiracists, to always tell true stories about race. See table 3.1 for examples.

TABLE 3.1: False Stories Versus True Stories

False Stories	True Stories
My race is better because people like me are smarter.	Race doesn't have anything to do with how smart you are.
My race is better because people like me were the founders of the United States.	At the United States' founding, Black Africans and Native Americans were prohibited from holding any positions of power, or even from having a say in what kind of country America would become. The United States was founded by people who also enslaved and oppressed non-White people. To say that one race is better than another because one race "discovered" America is also a false story. There were already people here: Native Americans.
My race is better because people like me are more beautiful.	There are beautiful people of all different races; it's not fair to say one kind of person is the most beautiful.

Classroom Activity

LEARNING ABOUT ANTIRACISM

As your students learn about White supremacy, systemic racism, and Whiteness, it's important to emphasize a path toward antiracism. The book, *Not My Idea: A Book About Whiteness* by Anastasia Higginbotham (2018) is a great resource for helping students understand how Whiteness operates to keep "good" White people "innocent," or untouched by racism, and ways to disrupt this pattern and break silences. The book is about a White child who learns about a shooting of an unarmed person of color. Depending on the age group you teach, you may need to prepare your students and families for the violence referenced in the book. A couple of pages include a picture of a handgun and a reference to the shooting.

Prior to reading the book, tell your students that this book is about a White child who learns about racial injustice in her community and decides to do something about it. The people around her are trying to shield her from this knowledge, not because they are bad people, but because they don't want her to be scared by it. As she reads about the history of White supremacy in the United States, she notices that people she loves have bias, and she decides to do something about it by learning about White antiracists and growing justice in herself.

This book offers a path forward for White children to develop strong, positive racial identities. Importantly, the best way to do that is to have role models, other White people who are dedicated to the work of antiracism.

Activities at the end of the book help students recognize that they don't have to accept White privilege and that White people contribute to social justice. After reading the book, spend some time on teaching White antiracists. This is important for all students to learn about, as it works against the myth that racism only affects people of color and should be solved by people of color, and the myth that change comes about through individual efforts of well-known activists like Dr. King rather than from diverse groups working together to solve big social problems. As a starting point, consider the following White antiracists and visit www.teachingwhilewhite.org/resources/white-antiracist-activists for more examples.

- **Sarah Moore Grimké (1792–1873) and Angelina Emily Grimké (1805–1879):** The Grimké sisters were speakers, writers, and educators. They were the first U.S. White female advocates for women's rights and the abolition of slavery.
- **Juliette Hampton Morgan (1914–1957):** A librarian and civil rights activist in Montgomery, Alabama, Morgan often spoke out against racism by writing letters to the *Montgomery Advertiser*. She was also known for pulling the emergency cord on public buses any time the White bus drivers treated Black passengers unfairly.
- **James Reeb (1927–1965):** A Unitarian minister and racial justice activist, Reeb participated in the Selma to Montgomery marches and a series of protests for African American voting rights. He was murdered by White segregationists for his activism.
- **Joan Trumpauer Mulholland (1941–):** As a teenager in the South during the civil rights movement, Mulholland was the first White person to join in the 1963 Woolworth's lunch counter sit-ins in Jackson, Mississippi. She also participated in

continued →

the March on Washington with Dr. Martin Luther King Jr. and a Selma to Montgomery march in 1965.

- **Chris Magnus (1960–):** Former police chief of Richmond, California, Magnus advocated for community policing and participated in Black Lives Matter protests alongside activists during his time as police chief in Richmond.

What can we do as teachers to avoid perpetuating false stories in the classroom? We can use our curriculum and classroom libraries to tell true stories about the strength and beauty of people who were left out of the narrative. Those of us who identify as White have a responsibility to be aware of White privilege and to actively work against any internal feelings of superiority and to fight against racism, bias, and prejudice at every turn. The following list suggests a few ways to do this.

- **Be on the lookout for bias and prejudice:** Speak out against it when you see it, whether in a book you are reading or listening to, in a movie, or among friends on the playground. This is one way to be an antiracist ally.
- **Check your own assumptions about people of color:** Practice saying to yourself, "You can't tell by looking." Grow your knowledge. Make sure you are always learning from and listening to diverse voices.
- **Take action:** Write letters, make signs, participate in Black Lives Matter actions. Use your voice to educate others.

Grow Justice in Ourselves

Elementary education has traditionally perpetuated a single story about racism: that a handful of influential people eradicated the bad racism of the past (Lee, Menkart, & Okazawa-Rey, 2002). Teachers celebrate Dr. King and praise the gains and positive changes our country made during the civil rights movement. While that is an essential and wonderful part of the story, it falls short of the whole truth. If we as teachers are to continue the powerful work initiated by antiracists of the past, we must also talk to students about ongoing racial injustice. We must empower them to recognize how White supremacy continues to exist and notice where the narrative of Whiteness persists. We must encourage them to learn from the many people of all races and ethnicities who are actively working toward these goals and to grow justice in themselves.

CHAPTER 4

DESIRE FOR A POST-RACIAL WORLD

Yet another reason White educators and parents give for not talking about race and racism is the desire to live in a world that looks beyond racial differences. When Barack Obama was elected the first Black president of the United States, the narrative of a post-racial society was born: "Perhaps America had turned far enough away from its racist past that skin color was no longer a barrier to the highest office of the land" (Hannah-Jones, 2016).

What allowed for the post-racial myth to flourish? Where does this desire for a world transcending race come from? I attended a workshop at Wisdom 2.0, a national mindfulness conference in San Francisco, in which the presenters spoke about the challenges they face as women and men of color in the mindfulness community. During the question-and-answer period, one of the White audience members asked the speakers to please stop speaking about their communities and begin to speak from the "I" perspective, so she could learn something about them as individuals. A very heated exchange followed, as the presenters tried to explain why the "we" matters, and that the woman's inability to understand their collective racial experience was a symptom of her privilege. The audience member was expressing her desire to speak "human to human" rather than to learn about race, power, and privilege. I see that woman's desire to form individual "human" bonds with people independent of race as a driving feature of the post-racial myth.

As one White parent told me when talking about her White children, "There's a part of me that loves that they see the friend or human first. I don't want to point out differences. . . . It's like a fear of ruining something precious."

In this chapter, we'll examine why parents want their children to adopt a color-blind ideology. Unfortunately, that approach does not prevent microaggressions in the classroom. Instead of accommodating this wish for erasing race, teachers can support students to notice and celebrate the ways we are all alike and different. Ultimately, teachers must go beyond a multicultural approach and adopt antibias education if they hope to address bias directly when it occurs. Classroom activities throughout the chapter will support you in integrating these lessons with students.

The Issue With Color Blindness

What's wrong with the idea of connecting human to human, independent of race? While it might seem well-meaning, it discriminates against people by erasing their identity. The desire for a world in which people don't see color is an ideology called *color blindness*. Professor of sociology Adia Harvey Wingfield (2015) explains why color blindness is problematic:

> [Many sociologists] argue that as the mechanisms that reproduce racial inequality have become more covert and obscure than they were during the era of open, legal segregation, the language of explicit racism has given way to a discourse of color blindness. But they fear that the refusal to take public note of race actually allows people to ignore manifestations of persistent discrimination. . . . By claiming that they do not see race, [Americans] also can avert their eyes from the ways in which well-meaning people engage in practices that reproduce neighborhood and school segregation, rely on "soft skills" in ways that disadvantage racial minorities in the job market, and hoard opportunities in ways that reserve access to better jobs for white peers.

Many White parents and educators who avoid talking about race are guided by this desire to develop a sense of color blindness in children. They may think a color-blind child is a more inclusive child or that color blindness allows the child to have a more authentic interaction with a child of a different race. But there are several major problems with the color-blind approach.

First, a person's unwillingness to see race devalues an important piece of another's identity. As a White parent of a first grader put it during one of the interviews I conducted with parents at my school:

> I had deluded myself into thinking that we live in a color-blind society, which I know is not true. So now I'm navigating that it's not even fair

> to people. Why would you want to be color blind? That's taking away something that's important.

Second, not everyone has the privilege of being colorblind. For some people, that's not a viable or realistic option. Consider non-White children in White majority classrooms who experience microaggressions, such as having their hair touched or being asked to speak on behalf of their race in the context of discussions about racial justice movements. In effect, the desire for color blindness has to do with collective history around race and racism and how Whiteness has been considered normal or, as some of my students used to say, "just regular."

Research on conscious and unconscious attitudes and beliefs about social identities has shown that African Americans and Asian Americans are less likely to be associated with the category "American" than their White peers. Researchers Thierry Devos and Mahzarin Banaji (2005) asked 135 undergraduates at Yale University to judge Whites, African Americans, and Asian Americans on their degree of "Americanness." Participants rated Whites more likely to embody the concept of "American" than Asian Americans and African Americans, even for those who were born in the United States and hold American citizenship (Devos & Banaji, 2005).

Ultimately, color blindness in the classroom is harmful because it denies very real differences that influence how students interact and treat one another and fails to create shared language and processes for addressing misunderstandings and discrimination when they arise. While some of the White parents I interviewed expressed pride that their child didn't say "my African American friend" or didn't talk about skin color differences at home, signifying to them that their child didn't see race, parents of color described events at school that made their children feel singled out and self-conscious. For example, parents of color talked about their children's frustrations when White classmates made comments about their hair or skin or singled them out in the conversation about the civil rights movement or Dr. King.

Microaggressions in the Classroom

The types of complaints parents of color report often involve microaggressions. *Racial microaggressions* are "brief and commonplace daily verbal, behavioral, or environmental indignities, whether intentional or unintentional, that communicate hostile, derogatory, or negative messages to target people based solely upon their marginalized group membership" (Sue et al., 2007). Some examples of microaggressions that frequently occur in elementary school classrooms are: White students touching or making comments about Black students' hair, White teachers mispronouncing names of students of color, and White teachers confusing students of color for one another.

The only way to combat microaggressions is to see them for what they are. A color-blind approach to the hair-touching microaggression, for example, would tell us to use general language around respect and courtesy to teach students not to touch their classmates' hair. But this doesn't always work, especially with very young children, who are often expressing curiosity about difference. A more effective approach is to talk openly about hair, how it's the same and different for everyone, what happens when we touch it, and why this is a problem. Some great resources to educate young students about hair are:

- **Learning for Justice's (n.d.d) lesson on hair entitled *Who Has Hair?***—This lesson helps students learn about how all mammals have hair and what is different and the same about hair.
- **Sandra Cisneros's *Hairs/Pelitos* (1997)**—This is a great book for teaching about the diversity of hair within families.
- ***I Love My Hair!* by Natasha Anastasia Tarpley (2001)**—Tarpley's book affirms natural Black hair, hair that has been devalued.

Deepen the learning by talking to your students about how important it is to affirm, learn about, and celebrate Black hair. If your class generated the "False Stories" list in chapter 3 (page 43), use this opportunity to add the false story that White hair is better, more beautiful, or more desirable than other types of hair. Students in grades K–2 can use puppets to act out what it would feel like to have someone say your hair is not as pretty as someone else's, or what it feels like to have unwanted hair touching. Students in grades 3–5 can have more nuanced discussions about how hair discrimination is a type of racial discrimination by discussing current or past events. As an example, students could learn about Mya and Deana Cook, twin sisters in Massachusetts who had to serve detention when school officials determined that their braids violated school policy (Lattimore, 2017).

White parents and educators may be hesitant to see microaggressions for what they are. But if we shift the focus to the experience of students, we must ask: What is the impact on young students of hearing their names mispronounced every day because their teachers have not made the effort to learn the correct pronunciation? Or being told they can't play with someone or join in a game because of their racial identity? Or their personal space and boundaries around their bodies repeatedly being disregarded? Shifting focus from intent ("He didn't mean it like that") to impact ("She was hurt by his words. How do we make it better, and make sure it doesn't happen again?") is one way to begin to honestly grapple with race and racism and how it plays out among young children.

Teachers are responsible for making the classroom a safe place for all students to thrive. A color-blind approach that perpetuates the post-racial myth will not support them in fulfilling that responsibility. As teachers practice talking about race, celebrating difference, and normalizing respect, microaggressions will diminish.

Classroom Activity

THE IMPACT OF OUCH MOMENTS

You can use the following activity, developed by Bret Turner (personal communication, June 2020), to introduce the concept of microaggressions to students in grades K–2, by talking about how certain *ouch moments*—times when others' words hurt us—can be more damaging than others.

First, read Tracy Hoexter's (2015) children's book, *A Wrinkled Heart*. Next, give each student a paper heart and instruct them to generate a list of unkind things others have said to them. After writing each statement, students can fold or wrinkle their paper hearts a little bit. Talk to the class about the impact of hurtful words, using the crushed heart as an illustration. Like the wrinkles in the heart, words leave a mark on our memories.

Next, read the book *Ouch! Moments: When Words Are Used in Hurtful Ways* by Michael Genhart (2015) about how hurtful words often carry meanings of which children aren't aware. Encourage students to look again at the list of hurtful words they wrote on their paper hearts and ask them to notice similarities and differences about the hurts.

When I completed a similar activity with my students, their list included everyday injustices of a kindergarten student, such as, "Someone took my spot in line," as well as more damaging hurts, such as, "Someone told me I couldn't play because I'm a girl." I asked my students to notice the hurts that were about parts of ourselves that are about who we are, or our identity. I told them that these ouch moments hurt more than others and are ones we all must especially

continued →

be on the lookout for, because they are about pieces of us that are damaging to who we are.

Finally, tell students that ouch moments related to identities are called *microaggressions*. You can also use the analogy of mosquito bites with your students; how getting multiple bites feels really bad, and that's what it feels like when microaggressions go unchecked. Figure 4.1 provides examples of microaggressions and sample responses that address the impact of the microaggression and ways to repair harm.

Microaggressions	*Example of a Response*
A White student says to a teacher when asked about the game she's playing, "We're playing hair salon. Anyone can play who has the right kind of hair."	Say, "Is it fair for you to decide what the 'right' kind of hair is? If your game excludes someone because of a difference, is it a fair game to play? How can you make this game fair?"
When a Black adult enters the classroom, a White student tells a Black student that their parent is here.	Say, "Remember, people of different races can be in the same family. There's no way to know by looking at someone who their parent is, or who their child is. Why else may this person be in the room? They could be a visiting teacher, a special guest, or an expert on an area we are studying."
A White student is drawing a picture of her classmates, and, while she's been carefully choosing different skin color markers for the White students in the class, decides to use the same skin color pencil for the Black students. She says, "They are just the same."	Say, "Remember, we are all the same and different from each other, and we can't tell by looking how someone identifies, or anything about them. How do you think it feels to have someone decide for you what your skin color is? What makes this unfair? How could you find out what skin color marker would be just right? You would have to ask your friends which marker they choose."

Figure 4.1: Examples of microaggressions.

Similarities and Differences

The color-blind approach carries an implicit message that if parents and teachers don't teach children to see color, they won't. But science doesn't confirm this belief. Research shows that babies begin to notice skin color differences as early as six months old and, as they become toddlers, become very interested in ideas of same and different (Winkler, 2009). In fact, students in early elementary grades are busy sorting their environment all the time and putting like with like.

I am fascinated by my kindergarteners' tendency, when given a bin of multicolored toys, to immediately sort the objects by color. Educators also ask students to sort every day in subjects such as mathematics or reading, to name common attributes of shapes and sort shapes by these commonalities, and to notice common word families and sort words by ending sounds. As educators, we recognize the value in the tendency to sort and organize, and we encourage our students to think deeply about core academic subjects. But when students attempt to organize and sort one another, teachers feel uncomfortable; they ask students to refrain from sorting and to pretend that the differences aren't there or to ignore them. The question to ask here is how we can encourage our students to think deeply about similarities and differences in one another, in the same way we do when teaching other academic subjects. What foundational understandings do they need to have about what makes us all similar and different?

By teaching about ways that people are alike and different—whether this means hair, skin color, family traditions, and others—teachers allow students to begin to grasp the complexity of identities and work against the false idea that rules can be applied to entire groups. Students begin to understand that to treat people fairly, they need to challenge their own assumptions and the assumptions of others. Ultimately, the goal is to help students learn how to treat all people fairly and in caring ways. As students learn that they can't apply rules to entire groups (whether these groups are girls, boys, racial groups, religious groups, or others), they also learn how important it is to take the time to get to know people, to know their individual stories.

At the beginning of each school year, as our class learns about each other, our families, and what makes a family a family, I show my students a photo of my family. I tell them that my daughters have a mom (me) who is White, and a dad who is Black, which is why their skin color is a mix of our colors. I usually share my family photo with them after we have read the book *All the Colors We Are* by Katie Kissinger (2014), a book that explains in simple terms where skin color comes from, so that they know the facts: skin color comes from the sun, melanin, and your ancestors. Then, we can have a conversation about diverse families, rather than a conversation to clear up confusion about skin color.

One year, one of my students, Clara, came up to me after our discussion and said, "Your kids don't look like you." I reminded her that they have one parent with dark skin and one with light, so they are a combination of both. She looked down and said, "I hate that I keep saying this, but they don't look like you." I realized then that my family confused her. She was used to seeing families where children had the same race as their parents. Not only did my daughters not have the same skin tone as either of their parents, but they were also different from each other.

The next day, I read the book *I Am Mixed* by Garcelle Beauvais and Sebastian A. Jones (2013), a beautiful book about biracial twins with different skin tones from one another, and I talked to the class about how the children in the book reminded me of my own children. We looked at many different family photos, of all different racial combinations, and talked about what made these families all the same ("They all have love") and what made them different ("They have different colored hair and different skin colors, and some have one parent").

We read *The Family Book* by Todd Parr (2003) for more examples of the diversity of family structures. All the while, I noticed that Clara kept looking over at my family photo. It occurred to me that my family may have been disrupting a rule she had in her mind for families, that the children's race necessarily matches their parents' race.

Finally, I put all the family photos the students had brought in on our board and asked the class to notice any patterns. "Four is the most!" one student offered. We'd counted the number of people in our families the day before, and four had been the most common number. "Anything else?" I asked. "They are all families," one student said. I nodded, and said, "You may also notice a pattern of skin color matching, or kids having the same skin color or race as their parents. That's a pattern you may see in this class sometimes, or out in the world, or in your own family, but that's not a rule. There's no rule that says children have to have the same race or skin color as their family." Emphasizing "That's a pattern, not a rule" is a helpful way to disrupt the tendency young students have of applying generalizations or rules to others, whether that be family structures, the types of jobs people have, or what's available to different genders.

According to antibias educators Louise Derman-Sparks and Julie Edwards (2010), for young students to develop a healthy sense of their own identities, they need the opportunity to explore similarities and differences with one another, and to begin to unlearn any forming biases or prejudices about these differences. In the second edition of their book, *Anti-Bias Education for Young Children and Ourselves*, the authors write (Derman-Sparks & Edwards, 2010):

> From infancy on, children notice and are curious about all kinds of differences among people. They also develop their own (often surprising) explanations for the differences that they observe and experience. By preschool, children have already developed ideas about many aspects of human diversity—including ideas that may seem quite strange to

> adults. Moreover, many children already have begun to develop discomfort about or even fear of specific kinds of differences. (p. 4)

This can be surprising for parents and educators, who may not know that toddlers and preschoolers are busy sorting and categorizing one another and the world around them based on these similarities and differences. The following classroom activities provide examples of how to address similarities and differences through instruction.

Classroom Activity

WINDOWS AND MIRRORS

Windows and mirrors is an approach to teaching and to diversifying children's literature, developed by Rudine Sims Bishop (1990), professor emerita of education at The Ohio State University and author of the seminal paper, "Mirrors, Windows, and Sliding Glass Doors." Bishop's idea is that all students need mirrors, or places at school where they see themselves reflected, and windows, places where they learn about others (McNair & Edwards, 2021).

When you teach about similarities and differences, ask your students to compare their similarities with others to the experience of looking in a mirror, which may feel familiar or known. In contrast, ask them to compare their differences with others to the experience of looking out of a window, which may bring out feelings of curiosity or wonder. This frame allows students to be curious about differences, which can lead to greater understanding, rather than be dismissive or judgmental, which can lead to bias or prejudice. It also works to challenge students to think critically about their assumptions, recognize what binds a community together, and identify traits they share with peers.

Point out that we have windows and mirrors with everyone. We may have a lot in common with people in our own families, for example, but there are also ways that we are different from them. In the same vein, we may seem very different from someone in another part of the world, but if we get to know them, we will find that we have commonalities too. Finding windows and mirrors with everyone works to build empathy and counters the idea that people can be categorized, or that you can assume you know everything about anyone. Instruct students to draw and write about their windows and mirrors with a

continued →

character in a class read-aloud or with one another. Students can also critically examine their classroom to make sure there are appropriate mirrors for everyone.

Classroom Activity

SAME, SAME BUT DIFFERENT

Read the book *Same, Same but Different* by Jenny Sue Kostecki-Shaw (2011) about two children who live in different parts of the world and are pen pals. After reading the story, draw a T-chart to compare and contrast the characters in the book. Label one side of the chart "Same" and the other side "Different," and have your students generate ideas about what makes these characters the same and what makes them different.

Instruct students in grades 3–5 to draw a Venn diagram with the names of the characters at the top. Students can generate character traits or attributes for each character and then think about what they have in common. Although these children live in different parts of the world, they have important things in common: they both like to climb trees, they both have pets, and they both go to school. Apply this idea, "same, same but different," to other discussions, especially about characters in books who may seem similar at first glance.

Classroom Activity

WE'RE DIFFERENT, WE'RE THE SAME

Read the book *We're Different, We're the Same* by Bobbi Jane Kates (1992), a book that explains, in simple terms, the difference between form and function. Each page begins with "We're different," and names body parts that are different in form for everyone, including noses, eyes, hair, and skin. The next page reads "We're the same," and explains how these parts of our bodies all serve the same function. This book helps young students begin to develop a scientific understanding of *how* we are the same and different, as well as a deeper appreciation of all that we have in common, even though we may look different from one another. After listening to the story, hand out small mirrors, and have your students draw self-portraits. They can share these self-portraits with one another at the end of the activity.

The Limits of a Multicultural Approach

As we move away from color-blind teaching, we talk openly about similarities and differences and celebrate how we are alike and different. As a result, our students start to appreciate and understand the diversity around them. But if our goals also have to do with teaching students to become antiracists, students who will work against individual prejudices and unfair systems, our teaching cannot stop there.

In the early years of teaching about Dr. King (page 77), I talked to students about the importance of celebrating differences, read them lots of diverse books, and emphasized the beauty and importance of diversity. In time, I came to understand that this is called a *multicultural approach.*

Teacher educator and author Zaretta Hammond defines *multicultural education* as "the 'Small World' approach, a celebration of diversity, what we usually see in schools" (as cited in Gonzalez, 2017). Multiculturalism includes learning about different holidays and languages or holding a food fair to celebrate different foods from around the world, or making sure students are reading books featuring diverse characters. While this approach ensures that all students see themselves reflected in the classroom and learn about people different from them, multiculturalism does not address what Hammond (2015b) calls *learning capacity,* a student's ability to access the learning and achieve success. In essence, diverse books, in themselves, don't magically create the conditions for success.

Hammond (2015a) suggests that educators and schools also apply a *culturally responsive* approach, one focused on improving the learning capacity of diverse students who have been marginalized educationally. Hammond (2015a) writes, "Culturally responsive teaching leverages the brain's memory systems and information processing structures." One way this works is by mimicking students' cultural learning styles and tools. Her book is an invaluable resource for any teacher or school leader interested in improving the conditions for student success.

To make lessons more culturally responsive, Hammond (2015a) suggests that teachers do the following.

- Turn lessons into games.
- Make the learning social through group learning activities.
- Allow students to *storify* the learning, which is to use new vocabulary in a narrative, rather than as part of a vocabulary test.

These are but a few examples. Hammond's (2015b) book *Culturally Responsive Teaching and the Brain* provides numerous strategies for effective culturally responsive teaching.

In time, I changed the way I taught about Dr. King's life and work (I expand on this in chapter 6, page 93). I extended my strategies beyond the multicultural approach, embraced culturally responsive teaching, and educated students about systemic racism and the roots of injustice. I owed it to my students to address biases and misconceptions they were forming about differences in our classroom community.

Antibias Education

In chapter 2 (page 29), I used Beverly Daniel Tatum's term *smog* to understand how racism infiltrates institutions through messages perpetuated in media. It's time to extend our learning as teachers to include bias because, as students internalize the smog, false ideas about race influence their ideas about one another, especially about people of color. *Biases* are beliefs that affect how individuals think, feel, and act toward others. They lead to acts of individual prejudice and discrimination. Starting in childhood, everyone absorbs and internalizes biases from larger societal attitudes (Derman-Sparks & Edwards, 2020).

To further understand the impact and danger of bias, it is helpful to consider the difference between explicit and implicit bias. *Explicit bias* is conscious prejudice—well-formed and clearly articulated degrading attitudes about others based on race. By contrast, *implicit biases* are attitudes or stereotypes that affect our understanding or decisions about others in an unconscious manner (Kirwan Institute for the Study of Race and Ethnicity, 2012). These attitudes develop over the course of a lifetime, are influenced by direct and indirect messages, and do not often align with our declared, or conscious, beliefs. Understanding implicit bias is especially important for people who attempt to treat everyone the same.

Isabel Wilkerson's (2020) discussion of caste illuminates how biases work in a culture to maintain a racial hierarchy. For Wilkerson (2020), casteism—any action or system that seeks to limit, hold back, or put someone in a defined ranking on the basis of a perceived category—is different from racism in that "good and kind people could be casteist, meaning invested in keeping the hierarchy as it is or content to do nothing to change it, but not racist in the classical sense, not active and openly hateful of this or that group" (p. 71). Kind people can still have biases or perpetuate an unjust system.

In the 1940s, psychologists Kenneth and Mamie Clark conducted experiments, known as "the doll tests," to understand how segregation affected Black children (NAACP Legal Defense and Educational Fund, n.d.). They asked the children to choose between dolls with dark skin and dolls with light skin. The results of this study showed an overwhelming preference for the White dolls. The findings were used in Brown v. Board of Education (1954), which led to the desegregation of schools. In 2010, CNN recreated a version of the doll tests in which White and Black children, ages four to five and nine to ten, were asked to identify certain characteristics such as "smart" or "good" by pointing to pictures of cartoon children that varied in skin color from light to dark (CNN, 2010). The White children overwhelmingly attributed positive attributes to the cartoons with light skin. The study also showed the Black children demonstrated an overall bias toward Whiteness. The results of this study deeply challenge the assumption that cross-racial friendships are authentic and don't require dialogue and examination.

What can teachers do to address such implicit bias in the classroom? The most effective way to combat bias is to adopt a proactive, or antibias, approach. This is especially important when it comes to implicit biases because they can easily go unchecked or unnoticed. Teachers can apply an antibias strategy, which includes engaging with students on many issues of identity development and what it means to be a respectful and equitable member of a diverse community.

Antibias education developed to identify and prevent the emotional and psychological effects of bias on students. Teachers and authors Derman-Sparks and Edwards (2020) explain the goals of antibias education:

> The goals are designed to strengthen children's sense of self and family (identity, Goal 1); to support their joy in human diversity (diversity, Goal 2); to enable them to gain the cognitive and social and emotional tools to recognize hurtful behavior (justice, Goal 3); and to develop the confidence and skills to work with others to build inclusive, fairer ways of being in a community (activism, Goal 4). (p. 20)

To foster a healthy identity development, students as young as preschool age need the opportunity to begin to un-learn any forming biases or prejudices about difference. These forming biases and prejudices can occur in the most well-meaning families, and they don't necessarily develop because of explicitly biased teachings; they can arise out of messages from the media, lack of exposure, or silence perpetuated by parents and educators. Recall my student who only thought about Black people in the context of poverty and homelessness. His parents hadn't told him that Black people were homeless, but they had remained silent on the subject of race and poverty. Derman-Sparks and Edwards (2020) go on to say:

> Some teachers and parents are not sure they should encourage children to "notice" and learn about differences among people. They think it is best to teach only about how people are the same, worrying that learning about differences causes prejudice. While well intentioned, this concern arises from a mistaken notion about the sources of bias. Differences, in and of themselves, do not create the problem. Children learn prejudice from prejudice—not from learning about human diversity. It is how people respond to differences that teaches bias and fear. (p. 46)

Children start forming biases early in life. Research suggests that babies as young as nine months old display same-race preferences. In a series of experiments, University of Toronto professor Kang Lee and colleagues (Xiao et al., 2017) showed nine-month-old infants photos representing different races and paired these faces with happy or sad music. The infants looked longer at people who shared their race paired with happy music, and people who didn't share their race paired with sad music. These results indicate that infants with exclusive experience with their own race develop associations between faces of their race and positive emotional experiences in the first year of life (Xiao et al., 2017). This research challenges the idea that if teachers and parents are careful not to say anything biased in front of children, they will not form biases themselves.

Other studies show that preschoolers begin to demonstrate racial bias by using racial categories as ways to exclude and include others and to negotiate power (Parker, Williams, & Steele, 2015). I remember a moment when my daughter experienced this at school. One afternoon as we sat together for an after-school snack, she reported, "Mommy, somebody said that only people with blue eyes could play the game."

"That doesn't sound fair," I said.

"No, it's not. I didn't want to play that game anyway," she concluded, scooting off her chair.

I held out my hand to hold onto hers. "It's never OK for anyone to say that to you," I said. "Or to anyone. I'm going to call the school right now so we can make sure everybody knows that, especially the person who said it."

She folded herself into a hug and then walked off to go find her sister. I called the school, and they contacted the family and talked to the student right away.

The blue-eyed student who told my daughter that she couldn't play was not necessarily being raised in a household that believed in excluding others based on differences. So, how had this bias developed? Research suggests that students' understandings of race are influenced by broader social norms, including power structures, and students are motivated to conform to these norms. Lawrence Hirschfeld (2012) compares the societal influence on a student's understanding of race to the way that they do (or don't) develop an accent. If the parents or caregivers were the sole influencers, we would expect all students' accents to mimic their parents' accents, but they don't. Instead, they develop normative speech patterns. To combat biases, or normative patterns, educators must be informed by antibias practices. Consider incorporating the following antibias activities into your classroom.

- **Create self-portraits:** When you discuss skin color with your students—after you've given them the facts about where skin color comes from: the sun, melanin, and your ancestors—have your students mix paint to find their skin tones and use this paint to decorate paper self-portraits. Add string for hair and more paint for the facial features. As your students explore their skin colors, emphasize the diversity in the room. Celebrate the differences among all the students, even those who share a racial identity, stressing that we are all the same and different. This understanding works against the bias expressed by some White students that all students of color look the same, as well as the bias around Whiteness being the norm or not a race.
- **Evaluate play materials:** Make sure the play materials and images on the walls reflect diverse identities. As Derman-Sparks and Edwards (2020) write, "when the dolls in the classroom are all White, or the pictures on the classroom walls show only White children, children can conclude that White is normal and other colors of

human skin are not as desirable" (p. 71). If you notice a pattern of students expressing preference for certain play materials over others (for example, the White dolls are chosen more than others), stress the beauty and value of the non-White dolls. One way to do this is to choose these play materials for a class presentation of some kind. In my class, we use our stuffed animals and dolls to help teach emotional literacy, such as feeling words, and other social-emotional lessons. Sometimes the students also put on puppet shows for the class. These are great opportunities to highlight non-White play materials.

- **Celebrate the color brown:** Read the book *Tan to Tamarind* by Malathi Michelle Iyengar (2009), a beautiful book of poetry dedicated to the color brown. Following the curriculum guide at the end of the book, hand out spices that are brown and let your students touch, smell, and taste them. Make art out of these spices or have your students write their own poems about brown. This combats biases forming against brown, a color often left out of children's poetry and songs.
- **Explore African cities and people:** Make sure to talk about Africa as a continent where people live, work, and learn, just like everywhere in the world. Show images of African cities and people, rather than animals and wildlife. This works against the bias that Africa is just a place for animals or that it's a place primarily for people who suffer. Teach about Dr. Wangari Maathai, who was the first African woman and first environmentalist to win the Nobel Peace Prize in 2004 for her work replanting trees in Kenya, as an example of the ingenuity and intelligence of the people from the continent.

Let's take a closer look at how to address bias directly when it occurs and what it might be like to diversify your classroom library.

Address Bias Directly When It Occurs

No matter how dedicated teachers are to antibias education or how careful they are in their approach to differences in the classroom, bias will sometimes occur. What do we do to address bias when it occurs in the classroom?

- Remember that moments of racial stress often require certain emotional regulation strategies (page 21). Locate where the stress is happening in your body, take deep breaths, and engage in positive self-talk.

- Address the bias head on. If a child says something disparaging about dark skin, respond immediately to correct the false narrative. For example, I've heard students say, "Dark skin is burnt" or "dirty." I typically respond by saying, "There's nothing burnt or dirty about dark skin. Remember, we learned that skin is darker because of melanin, the sun, and where people's ancestors come from." Helping your students access their prior learning can remind them of what they already know about differences.
- Notice the impact of the bias and work to solve any problems that arise as a result. This could sound like, "What you said was untrue, and it hurt your friend. What can we do to make it better?"

Diversify Your Classroom Library

When Marley Dias was ten years old, she embarked on a mission to collect one thousand books with Black girls as main characters and send them to a school in Jamaica that her mother had attended (Dias, n.d.). Dias was frustrated that the books she was assigned in school only featured White people, especially White boys, and she was aware that these were some of the same books teachers had assigned her great-grandparents to read (Schoinas, 2020). She wanted to read books that featured Black girls. As she said in an interview with *Forbes*, "I'm working to create a space where it feels easy to include and imagine Black girls and make Black girls like me the main characters of our lives" (as cited in McGrath, 2017). She launched her initiative, #1000BlackGirlBooks in 2016, and by 2019, she had collected over twelve thousand books. Her program continues to supply books that feature Black female characters to libraries, schools, and community organizations.

Dias's story reminds us of the danger of taking a color-blind approach to developing curricula and building classroom libraries. In truth, there is no such thing as a color-blind approach. Historically, the people who decided which books to assign to students and which influential figures to teach in social studies and history classes did not consider the value of diverse representations and neglected to include books from diverse authors.

The Cooperative Children's Book Center at the School of Education at the University of Wisconsin–Madison (2020) reports that in 2019, of 4,035 books collected, only 12 percent feature Black main characters, 9 percent Asian main characters, 6 percent Latinx main characters, and less than 2 percent Indigenous, Pacific Islander, and Arab main characters. If educators don't apply an antiracist lens and reject a color-blind ideology to the kinds of books they offer students, these trends will never change. To learn more about diversifying your classroom library, I recommend the following resources.

- We Need Diverse Books (https://diversebooks.org)
- Lee and Low Books (www.leeandlow.com)
- Teaching for Change (www.teachingforchange.org)

In 2020, Dias collaborated with Netflix on their new live action series *Bookmarks: Celebrating Black Voices* (Collins et al., 2020), in which she appears as the host and serves as an executive producer. Each episode features a children's book about the Black experience written by a Black author and read aloud by a Black celebrity. When I introduced Marley Dias, her mission, and her Netflix series to my students, I asked them how they would explain the problem Marley Dias is trying to solve. One of my students said, "We're talking about racism. When all the books are about White people, that's a part of racism." I couldn't have said it better.

Celebrate the Ways We Are Different

Most parents and teachers are united in their desire for students to live in a peaceful and just world. We create that world together, not by turning a blind eye to our differences but by seeing, understanding, and celebrating them. Teachers must find creative and compassionate ways to help students acknowledge and appreciate the similarities and differences within their classroom community, commit to kind and respectful engagement, and interrupt bias when it occurs.

PART TWO

Effective and Appropriate Ways to Talk About Race and Racism in Your Classroom

When we think about education, and how we are preparing young people to connect across lines of difference, so that they are able to function effectively in a diverse democracy, then we have to think about what we are doing in the classroom to encourage young people to develop these social skills.

—Beverly Daniel Tatum

In part one, I made a case for why teachers should talk to their students about race and racism. We examined four reasons people stay silent about race and why breaking the silence is a teacher's best tool for interrupting racism and equipping students to become changemakers.

In part two, I share my story of how I started speaking with my students about race and racism in the classroom. You'll read about the challenges I encountered along the way, the action steps I took to overcome those challenges, the changemaker curriculum my team and I developed, and how I involved parents and caregivers in the process. Finally, you'll get the chance to imagine undertaking this work for yourself by identifying potential roadblocks and how to work through them on your way to introducing antiracist practices into your classroom.

CHAPTER 5

THE IMPORTANCE OF SPEAKING UP

One of my favorite things about teaching five- and six-year-olds is the immediacy of their emotions and how readily they express their feelings. Kindergarten students make it difficult to ignore what's really happening for them, whether it be a rough night's sleep, an ongoing conflict with a friend, or frustration about some aspect of the academic program. My best teaching moments arise when I stay with what's happening in the moment for my students, rather than pushing ahead with my own agenda. Sometimes this means slowing down a writing unit to make sure that all the students are gaining the skills and competencies they need or speeding up a mathematics unit because they've grasped the concepts and are ready for more. Often, this means differentiating lessons based on individual student needs.

Early in my teaching career, I felt good about the classroom community I built year to year. It was rare that I didn't feel a connection with a student, or a family, or that I felt I hadn't gotten to know and appreciate each of my students. At the end of each year, I hoped and imagined that I'd successfully created a caring, bonded class community. One afternoon, though, I realized there was a gap in my teaching, areas of instruction and discussion I hadn't touched, and that this oversight was limiting my students' ability to bond with one another and with me in a truly respectful, inclusive way.

In this chapter, I'll share the story of realizing that I needed to change how I taught about Dr. King's life and work. After a crisis moment, I understood I needed to learn how to teach explicitly about race and racism. I'll recount the four major challenges my team and I faced and the action steps we took to address them.

My Story of Teaching About Race and Racism

It was a sunny afternoon in January 2010, the Friday before a long weekend to celebrate the work of Dr. Martin Luther King Jr. I held the book *Happy Birthday, Martin Luther King* by Jean Marzollo (2006) in my lap as I waited for my students to come in from lunch. I had been teaching kindergarten for a couple of years, so this wasn't the first time I would be reading a book about Dr. King to my students.

At the time, my daughters were nearing school age, and I had begun to wonder about what their experience would be like in school, especially around conversations about Dr. King, race, and racism. In that moment, though, I wasn't thinking about any of that. I was thinking about how excited I was to read to students about someone I'd always admired, whose work exemplified so many of my own values: taking nonviolent direct action, organizing, standing up for what you believe in, working for peace and justice.

I was aware that some students felt more connected than others to their peer group (and to me) and that there were social and academic issues that needed my attention. But until that day, it hadn't occurred to me that something fundamental was missing from my teaching, and that it was disrupting my students' ability to bond respectfully with one another. Until that day, I thought that teaching general lessons around identifying and understanding emotions and resolving conflict would allow my young students to interact inclusively with one another.

I thought that talking in general terms about peace and justice would allow my students to access and internalize these complicated concepts. I didn't yet understand that my students needed to learn about race and racism, as well as other differences, what they mean, and how to interact respectfully across them. I didn't yet know they needed repeated time and exposure to the themes I wanted them to grasp, and they needed multiple opportunities to make this learning personally meaningful.

As I opened the book that afternoon, I suddenly became hyper aware of my two Black students in the room. In hindsight, I see this as a flash of insight that the class should have had exposure to foundational learning before we talked about Dr. King. We were beginning this conversation in the wrong place. We hadn't read any picture books about race or skin color. We hadn't had any conversations about what the terms White and Black meant, let alone *segregation* or *boycott*. This was their first exposure in my classroom to the mention of race and protest movements. I knew that was wrong somehow, that my students should have had time to explore these concepts prior to hearing this story. I sensed things were going to go downhill.

When I read a page about the Montgomery bus boycott, a White student at my feet said, "That's like Matthew! He wouldn't be able to sit on the front of the bus!" I glanced over at Matthew, one of the Black students in the classroom. He looked back at me, quiet, waiting. I didn't know how to respond to the White student's comment. All I knew was I wanted this lesson to be over as quickly as possible, and I didn't want the whole class to suddenly look at Matthew and talk about him as if he weren't there. I was worried my White students were suddenly seeing Matthew in a new light, and I had no idea how to guide them through this noticing in a way that would support Matthew. I didn't know how to foster my students' understanding about race and racism. I closed the book before finishing it, and said, "Isn't it great we can be together now?"

With that statement, I sent a message to my students that racism was a thing of the past. In fact, I hadn't uttered the word racism, so what they had gotten from that first reading about Dr. King was that there used to be an exclusion problem, but the problem was solved. I could sense this wasn't right, that it didn't go far enough. I knew that racism isn't actually a thing of the past, that it still happens, but in the moment I didn't know how to convey that to my students.

The subsequent activities I chose reinforced this message. We drew ourselves on a bright yellow bus and hung it up in the room. We thought about our dreams, wrote and drew them on paper clouds, and hung these up as well. The dreams were often not about race or racism at all, but general ideas around inclusivity, or even fantastical dreams that had nothing to do with the larger themes around social justice I had hoped to communicate. I remember leaving the classroom that day feeling frustrated and worried. I was surprised at how nervous I had been to tell this story to my students. I realized I was afraid that talking about the truth of racism would divide my class rather than unite it. I was worried that Matthew had left my classroom feeling singled out. I was deeply aware of his silence that day.

The next day, I tried again. I had not finished the book the previous day, after the White student's comment about Matthew. So, I picked it up and continued to read. When I got to the page about Dr. King's assassination, I paused, realizing I didn't know if I wanted to tell this part of the story to my five- and six-year-old students. Many thoughts rushed through my head: *Do any of my students know about this already? What do their parents want them to know? Is this too scary for young students?*

Before I read the page, one student called out, "He was shot! He's dead!"

Suddenly, the room buzzed with the topic of Dr. King's murder. I was uncomfortable with this truth being leaked out in this way, and I didn't know how to manage the information. I quickly finished the book and changed the subject.

I wasn't proud of my teaching; I knew that my students had not even begun to grasp the larger themes I cared so much about. And because I had no idea how to teach around this topic that would lead to greater understanding, I stopped teaching about it altogether.

The following year, I dreaded the day I was scheduled to read about Dr. King because I sensed the events of the previous year would repeat themselves: White students would talk about students of color, and the topic of Dr. King's death would be the most salient to the students. That's exactly what happened. I had all the same feelings; I was preoccupied by frustration, worry, and a deep disappointment in my ability to teach this the right way. I wanted to cover this topic in a way that would produce the results I wanted: I wanted all my students to understand the importance of changing unfair systems and practices with nonviolent direct action. I wanted them to recognize the evils of racism. But as the same troubling events unfolded, I retreated once again into safer teaching topics.

In the fall of 2011, my daughter entered kindergarten at my school, and she was the only biracial Black and White student in her class. On the day that her teacher read a book about Dr. King to the class, she brought the book home with her and showed it to me. My daughter stopped me near the end of the book on a page that contains a drawing of a Black girl staring out at the reader.

She rested her hand on the photo of the child and said, "And that's when everyone in my class pointed at her."

"At the girl in the story?" I asked. She nodded and motioned for me to continue reading.

Although I didn't think my daughter's classmates had pointed at her that day, I sensed that she was telling me something about how it felt to be the only Black student in her classroom as they learned about Dr. King.

Hearing my daughter share her experience, I felt a new sense of urgency. I had to make this better for her and for other students of color who were in the minority in their classrooms.

The following day, at our weekly staff meeting, teachers shared how our conversations about Dr. King were going in our classrooms. A second-grade teacher said of one of her White students, "He talked about how Matthew wouldn't have been at this school if our school was segregated." She went on to say she thought this student had gained a deep appreciation of the injustice of the time by making a personal connection to his Black classmate. But this was the same Matthew who had been singled out and talked about in my classroom.

At that moment, I realized that there were students at our school who were having the same experience year after year, in January, when every teacher read a book about Dr. King. Coupled with my own daughter's experience of feeling "pointed at," this spurred me to action. Something had to change. I couldn't let this pattern continue. I had to find a way to change my comfort level. I had to grow my understanding of how to teach about race and racism in a way that would be inclusive of all voices, prevent students from being singled out, and equip students to talk and think about standing up against injustice and using nonviolence to create change.

In time, I did find a way to teach my students about race and racism, though it came with difficulty. The following sections detail a series of challenges I faced along the way as well as action steps I took to address each challenge.

Challenge: Limited Dialogue With Colleagues

I knew I would have to start talking about what was happening in my classroom with my colleagues. This required letting go of any fixed idea about what kind of teacher I was, or what kind of classroom I was able to create year to year. I had to admit there was a problem that I didn't know how to solve by myself. This was difficult, especially considering my values around teaching about social justice and creating a caring class community. It helped to remember any discomfort I was feeling about this experience was much less important than the potential positive outcomes of transforming what was happening in my classroom.

Fortunately, I learned that my colleagues on the kindergarten teaching team were equally disturbed by similar experiences in their classrooms. During our weekly planning meetings, we shared our observations of our students and talked openly about what was troubling us. The following are a few examples of the kinds of issues that came up during these meetings.

- One teacher shared that it made her uncomfortable whenever a White student said, in a conversation about school segregation, "Those kids wouldn't be able to go to *my* school." These kinds of comments, however innocently uttered, can cause real harm by perpetuating a system in which Whiteness is superior. In effect, the White student who uses terms like "my school" is communicating to non-White students that the school doesn't belong to them.

- Another teacher said she didn't know how to get her students to move on from talking about the assassination, as if nothing else about Dr. King mattered.
- Another wondered aloud how to give students an accurate sense of time, as several of her students over the years had wondered if Dr. King had been alive with the dinosaurs. For these students, it was as if he'd lived "too long ago to count."

As we all faced this challenge together, we wondered how to make changes without causing harm to students of color in our classrooms. As a transitional kindergarten teacher put it, "How do I have this conversation with my students in a way that doesn't make the White students look at the Black students in a new way, and not a positive one?" Derman-Sparks and Ramsey (2011) frame the question in this way: "[What are the ways] to help students unlearn racism without harming those who are the targets of racism?" (p. 135). Consider the following recommendations.

- Address moments of bias when they occur. Treat them as teachable moments.
- Use persona dolls. Give these classroom dolls a name, birth date, family, likes, dislikes, and so on that remain as constant as those characteristics do for real children in the classroom. Use these dolls to act out scenarios of exclusion based on difference, long before you begin talking about racism and other systems of oppression. In chapter 6 (page 93), I offer sample scripts and lessons for role playing with puppets or persona dolls.
- Allow students to practice identifying the feelings that are often a result of exclusion (anger, sadness, loneliness, frustration) and empathize with these feelings. Giving students the opportunity to identify, name, and understand difficult emotions surrounding injustices such as racism allows them to build empathy for those affected, as well as gain a deeper understanding of the negative impact of engaging in exclusionary behavior.

To increase White students' understanding of race and racism, decrease the harm done to students of color, and promote positive identity development,

Derman-Sparks and Ramsey (2011) offer seven learning themes for White students. Table 5.1 lists these themes and offers suggested activities to address each one.

TABLE 5.1: Learning Themes for White Students

Learning Theme	Suggested Activity
"Develop authentic identities based on personal abilities and interests, family history and culture, rather than on White superiority" (p. 61).	Get to know your students by having them bring in All About Me bags, filled with special objects and a family photo. Give each student a chance to share their All About Me bag with the class, and have each student draw a picture after these presentations, in which they draw several things they learned about their classmates.
"Know, respect, and value the range of the diversity of physical and social attributes among White people" (p. 62).	Have your students draw a self-portrait. On the back of the paper, have them dictate or write one thing about themselves you couldn't tell by looking at them. When you share these with the class, emphasize all the things we can't tell by looking: favorite foods, music, family traditions, and others.
"Build the capacity for caring, cooperative, and equitable interactions with others" (p. 62).	Make a class book about how your students are helpers for others; the sentence starter could be "I am a helper when I . . ." Provide opportunities for cooperative work and play, such as a group mural or building project.
"Understand, appreciate, and respect differences and similarities beyond immediate family, neighborhood, and racial group" (p. 125).	Using windows and mirrors as a repeated frame, ask your students to list or draw similarities and differences with multiple people. For family members, you can have them generate two or three ways they are the same, and five ways they are different. Ask them to think of people they see as being very different from them, and have them list or draw more similarities than differences.

continued →

"Learn to identify and challenge stereotypes, prejudice, and discriminatory practices among themselves and in the immediate environment" (p. 126).	Have your students help you take inventory of your classroom library to identify any biases or stereotypes, or lack of representation of people of color. Ask them, "Why is this a problem? How can we solve it?" Include your students in diversifying and making more equitable the books provided. Alternatively, have your students write letters to companies that they have identified aren't fairly representing people of color.
"Commit to the ideal that all people have the right to a secure, healthy, comfortable, and sustainable life and that everyone must equitably share the resources of the earth" (p. 126).	Highlight contributions of people of color (as scientists, inventors, engineers, artists) and your students' awareness of the range of roles people of color carry out. Use community building experiences (field trips, special guests) to challenge assumptions White children can make about people of color, and to expand awareness.
"Build identities that include antibias and multicultural ideals and possibilities and acquire the skill and confidence to work together for social justice" (p. 127).	Create posters and murals that affirm antiracist values. Visit Learning for Justice's (n.d.a) Art and Activism lesson for ideas on how to integrate art with social justice teaching (www.tolerance.org/classroom-resources/lessons/art-and-activism). Have your students educate the wider school community about a current issue that needs solving and ways to take action to solve it.

Source: Derman-Sparks & Ramsey, 2011.

Challenge: Not Clearly Identifying Problem Areas

A major factor our team recognized early on was that we were not clearly identifying the problem areas in our classroom. White students made troubling statements during conversations about the civil rights movement. There were gaps in students' understanding of race. We weren't yet teaching efficiently about racism. We noticed these trends, but we hadn't yet articulated the specific problems that gave rise to them. This was an essential step we had to take in order to find ways to address these problems and, eventually, make fundamental changes to our teaching practice.

My colleagues and I decided we needed to clarify the problems we were observing and share them with the larger school community. We identified three key issues:

1. White students were singling out students of color in conversations about race and racism. This was the most immediately concerning problem to me.
2. We were starting this story in the wrong place, and our students were missing important pre-learning around topics like exclusion versus inclusion and nonviolence as a strategy for change—topics that would improve their understanding of Dr. King's work and the ongoing work of antiracist movements.
3. We needed to understand what was developmentally appropriate to share with five- and six-year-olds, which brought up a question about what teachers in other grades were doing and why. We ended these meetings with the conviction that our school needed a scope and sequence to this work, similar to how we plan for literacy and mathematics units, so that each teacher at every grade could know what their students needed to know by the end of that grade, and teaching would build on the work done in previous years.

Around this time, I was serving as diversity and inclusion team leader for kindergarten through fourth grade, which meant that I met frequently with the diversity director and the middle school team leader to address issues that were arising on both campuses and to plan staff development trainings. We were in the process of developing a series of trainings that would allow faculty and staff to work in advocacy groups to learn more about an issue that they cared about and that impacted our community. These trainings included talking and teaching about socioeconomic class, religion, gender, race, learning differences, and how we teach about Dr. King and the civil rights movement. Over the course of the year, we met in these advocacy groups to research our topics and decide what we wanted our colleagues to know or do. My group had middle school teachers as well as elementary school teachers, which was helpful in gaining more clarity about what eighth graders were able to say about Dr. King by the time they graduated. In our final meeting, we came up with our enduring understandings for this teaching. Following is a sample of six enduring understandings.

1. Learn about differences rather than judge them or make assumptions about them.
2. Learn strategies to make a difference. (Teach strategies to empower students to take action.)
    a. Be courageous.
    b. Take an uncomfortable risk when you see unfairness.
    c. Use your words.
3. Recognize that human rights struggles are ongoing.
4. Remember that diverse multiracial, multiethnic groups work together to make change. (White people work for social justice as well. It is important to know that White people work against racism, specifically. And it's important to know that people of color work for other kinds of justice, as well.)
5. Make a personal connection to social justice (at home and school).
6. Seek historical accuracy.

To begin a collaborative, or personal, investigative process into your teaching practice about race and racism, visualize how you wish the lessons and conversations would go and write down what you hope students say or ask. Alternatively, imagine what you would want your young students to know and say about race and racism when they graduate from your school. This could sound like, "My students will be able to identify racist practices and beliefs, confront them in the moments that they occur, and live a life committed to antiracism." These visualizations will help you clarify what you want your learning goals or essential understandings to be. From there, you can backward plan in a thoughtful and informed way and integrate these learnings into several areas of your curriculum, rather than limit them to a single or several isolated lessons about Dr. King.

For example, if you decide you want your students to know how to combat bias, you might decide to teach lessons on bias that include defining the term and giving them multiple opportunities to identify biases as well as opportunities to speak out against it. You could decide you want your students to role-play different scenarios and practice language that combats bias, such as, "What you said isn't true, and it's not fair," or identify biases in a story and have a class conversation about what the students would do or say if they were in the book.

Use the following six questions as a starting point to investigate your teaching practice:

1. What are the themes that matter the most to me about this topic?
2. How can I weave these themes into other areas of the curriculum?
3. Where and how am I already highlighting these themes in my teaching?
4. What knowledge or understandings do I want my students to gain from the lessons and conversations?
5. What do I want my students to be able to do differently as a result of the lessons and conversations?
6. Given the skills and strategies I want my students to have, how can I develop multiple lessons that will teach the knowledge and understandings I have decided are important?

Challenge: No Scope and Sequence

At the time that we were investigating our approach to teaching about Dr. King, race, and racism, we didn't have an established scope and sequence. We needed a scope and sequence to guide our investigation and allow us to spot holes, gaps in instructions, or places where we were repeating books and lessons. In contrast, when we wanted to know if our writing program was preparing students to be the kind of writers we wanted them to be, we could check various documents (information on our website, internal grade curriculum guides, or our established curriculum) and find out what students learned at each grade level. Not having a predetermined curriculum on Dr. King required us to collect a significant amount of data, including finding out which books teachers read in every classroom and what activities they led. While this was time consuming, it allowed us to continually ask ourselves what we wanted students to know by the time they graduated and to view the data we collected through the lens of our essential goals. The scope and sequence that eventually came out of this work reflected our emphasis on these goals.

Our scope and sequence to the work around teaching about Dr. King and the civil rights movement is a K–8 study of changemakers. In kindergarten, teachers talk about what it takes to be a changemaker, introduce social and environmental movements, identify key leaders in these movements, and guide students to find changemakers in their own communities. Students revisit this study in each grade. For example, first graders focus on labor organizers, and third graders study Indigenous activists, culminating in an eighth-grade final project where they interview a changemaker, create a teaching poster, and present their changemaker to the school community and families. In addition, each year the student council honors school alumni who are changemakers in their communities. The finalists visit the school and present their work to current students in an assembly, often sharing that the inspiration for their initiatives began at Prospect Sierra School.

To begin the process of developing a scope and sequence at your school, identify colleagues who will readily start this work with you as well as members of the school administration. Together, identify your key learning outcomes and goals, and develop a plan for collecting necessary information from teachers at each grade level. If you are approaching this work alone, make a list of your personal goals in your own teaching practice, and connect these goals to other areas of learning. If your school has adopted a formal social-emotional learning program, or has dedicated instructional time to these efforts, connect goals around teaching about race and racism to this curriculum. This could sound like, *I want my students to interact respectfully with one another and be kind to one another—two of the foundational goals of our social-emotional learning program. In order for my students to develop this kind of respect, they need to understand similarities and differences they share with members of our classroom and the larger community surrounding our school so they are not developing bias or prejudice. My goal in this work is to reduce bias and prejudice, which involves talking about race and racism.* Present these goals to interested colleagues and school leaders.

Challenge: Only Discussing Dr. King When Teaching About the Civil Rights Movement

As I collected data around how our K–4 teachers were approaching Dr. King's birthday and the civil rights movement, I began to notice a pattern. We were reading the same books year after year and focusing primarily on Dr. King's story. I wondered how we could ever get to broader understandings—for example, that social change is the work of many people over generations, rather than the lifetime of a single historical figure—if we weren't teaching about other people involved in the movement, including modern-day activists. I worried that our teaching was perpetuating the hero myth (the idea that change comes about because of special individuals), which can skew students' ability to appreciate the complexity and power of social movements and hinder them from finding their own way into the work.

I decided to conduct a schoolwide project on the civil rights movement, whereby I would ask teachers in grades K–4 to teach about someone other than Dr. King so that students could start to appreciate the complexity of the work. We needed to give them the opportunity to see that many people work together over time to create social change and that the work continues today. When we teach about multiple people, including people who are still alive, students can identify with these activists and see a path forward for themselves. The following list includes people we highlighted.

- **Claudette Colvin:** A Black teenager who also refused to give up her seat on a bus; she was the first to do so (Hofstaedter, n.d.)
- **Robert P. Moses:** A Black man who worked with the Greenwood Voter Registration Project to register African American voters in Mississippi (American RadioWorks, n.d.)
- **Thurgood Marshall:** A Black civil rights lawyer who served as chief attorney for the plaintiffs in Brown v. Board of Education (1954) (LDF Director-Counsels, n.d.) and later as the first Black Supreme Court justice
- **Bayard Rustin:** A Black leader in the civil rights movement who served as Dr. King's adviser; in 1957, Rustin was a founder of the Southern Christian Leadership Conference, a major force organizing the civil rights movement and March on Washington (Infoplease, n.d.)
- **Margaret Gunderson:** A White teacher at Japanese internment camps (Watanabe, 2005)
- **Jack Greenberg:** A White civil rights lawyer who worked with Thurgood Marshall (Learning for Justice, n.d.c)
- **John Lewis:** A Black leader of the civil rights movement, chairman of the Student Nonviolent Coordinating Committee (SNCC), and U.S. congressman since 1987 (Ibiblio, n.d.b)
- **Horace Julian Bond:** A Black social activist and leader of the civil rights movement; Bond was one of the founders of the SNCC and served as communications director of the SNCC and chairman of the NAACP from 1998–2009 (NAACP, n.d.)
- **Myles Horton:** A White educator and co-founder of Highlander Folk School in Tennessee, now the Highlander Research and Education Center, which ignored segregation laws and allowed people of all races

to study together in the 1950s and 60s; Horton was a friend of Rosa Parks and Martin Luther King Jr. (Milliarium Zero, 2011)

- **Ella Baker:** A Black organizer for Dr. King's Southern Christian Leadership Conference; Baker also ran a voter registration campaign called Crusade for Citizenship (Ibiblio, n.d.a)
- **Laurie Olsen:** A White woman who serves as director of California Tomorrow, an organization devoted to helping immigrant students (Learning for Justice, n.d.c)
- **Vine Deloria Jr.:** A Native American writer and professor who addressed stereotypes of Indigenous people and challenged White audiences to take a new look at the history of U.S. westward expansionism; he was also a prominent figure in the struggle for Native American rights (Lowman & Barker, n.d.)

Your Response to Resistance

Most teachers were cooperative and enthusiastic about making changes to the way they taught about the civil rights movement and Dr. King, though I did have one White teacher ask me after a staff meeting why I was forcing other teachers to teach *my* curriculum. I was taken aback, as I did not feel like this curriculum belonged to me or that I was forcing it. I had assumed everyone would be equally as willing to reflect on a piece of curriculum that didn't seem to be doing what we wanted it to do and make necessary changes. I realized then that not everyone thought there was a problem, not in the same way I saw it. As a teacher with many years of experience, she felt satisfied that her students were getting what she wanted them to when they talked about Dr. King, a hero of hers.

As teachers, we are often asked to do more, take on a new initiative, change a piece of the curriculum, or adopt an entirely new program. This can feel overwhelming and sometimes unnecessary. I've thought a lot about that teacher's comment, especially in relation to times I haven't been immediately onboard with change. Change can be uncomfortable and challenging. It helps to remember that change is necessary, especially when student outcomes are not what we want them to be, and that it's not always about doing more, but doing something in a different, more effective way. Table 5.2 provides some responses to potential challenges to change.

TABLE 5.2: Challenging Comments and Productive Responses

Challenging Comments	*Productive Responses*
"I have too much to do. I wish I could do this, but I don't have the time."	"The hard part is taking inventory of what we are doing now and setting goals for what we want to occur because of this teaching. It's not so much a matter of doing more, but doing the work effectively. How would you feel if the issue were about improving below-grade-level reading or math performance?"
"This feels too personal. Shouldn't we leave it up to families to have the kinds of conversations they'd like to have at home about race and racism?"	"When we leave conversations about race and racism up to families, research tells us that not all families are talking about race and racism. White families don't tend to initiate conversations but are often receptive to following the cues of their educational institutions."
"My young students aren't ready for this. I'm focusing on teaching them how to be students!"	"Research tells us that young students are noticing differences and picking up on societal biases about these differences. Part of teaching them how to be students is giving them foundational instruction on race and how racism operates in our society so that they can be equipped with the tools to be inclusive and antiracist."
"I think what I'm doing now is working."	"How do you know? Do you have set goals for your instruction? Have you taken formal or informal assessments?"

I left that staff meeting feeling rattled but determined to stay focused on my goal: to transform the way I taught about race, racism, and Dr. King so that all my students would grasp the big ideas and themes I wanted them to, and no one would be singled out. As I closed up my classroom at the end of that year, I felt a new sense of purpose and excitement. I hoped the work we'd done would have the kind of impact I wanted it to. I had a list of books to read over the summer and some sample lesson plans to create. I was ready to get to work.

CHAPTER 6

PEACEFUL CHANGEMAKERS

My approach to teaching about Dr. King has evolved into teaching about race and racism generally, which begins in September as a foundational part of what happens in my classroom. Now I understand that my students need to know and understand how they are similar and different from one another—racially and in terms of gender, family structure, language, and so on—*long before* we begin talking about racism. They also need multiple experiences with big ideas around social justice and nonviolence as a strategy for change and direct learning about ongoing movements for racial and social justice, including the Black Lives Matter movement. Now, I recognize the value of including families in this learning from the very beginning, so that there are no surprises about what's happening in my classroom, and I can learn from parents and caregivers what values they stress at home and what my students know or don't know about the topic coming into kindergarten.

This knowledge did not hit me all at once but was a multi-year process of learning new things, such as how to integrate changemakers throughout my curriculum, trying these out, and critically examining what happened as a result from the vantage point of what I wanted to happen. I didn't want anyone to be singled out in conversation. I wanted my students to gain a beginning understanding of how social movements work and see a path forward for themselves in this work.

In this chapter, I will focus primarily on the first part of this change, the Peaceful Changemaker Curriculum my team and I developed. We introduced peaceful changemakers, read Tony Johnston's *Isabel's House of Butterflies*, chose an action project, and used persona dolls to introduce exclusion. When it came time to learn about Dr. King, I could tell we had made a lot of improvement, but I also noticed gaps in their learning that showed me our curriculum was still a work in progress.

Learning About Peaceful Changemakers

As a starting point, I realized I needed to build my own understanding of how young students learn about social justice and civil rights. Through reading "Learning about Holidays and Fairness" from Derman-Sparks and Edwards's (2020) *Anti-Bias Education for Young Children and Ourselves*, I learned that the most effective way to teach these themes is to do the following.

- Make them personal for children.
- Integrate them into other aspects of the curriculum so that they are not stand-alone lessons that only happen once a year.
- Ensure they are not only about one person—who may no longer be living.

Teaching about Dr. King as the hero of the civil rights movement, while ignoring the countless other people who worked alongside him (and before him and after him), teaches students that social movements are about individuals, rather than about diverse groups working together. In turn, this reinforces myths around individuality over community efforts. When students learn about other people involved, they understand that social movements comprise many kinds of people of all different ages, genders, and races, coming together to make big changes. This conveys the power of diversity, allows students to make personal connections, and sends the message that the work is ongoing. It doesn't stop with one person's death.

To learn about other people involved in the civil rights movement, I read Taylor Branch's (1989, 1998, 2007) books on the United States during the time of Dr. King, extensive works that tell the stories of numerous people of different races and ages.

As a result, I sought ways to integrate the themes of social justice and nonviolence as strategies for change into other areas of our curriculum. In kindergarten, much of our social studies work is around habitat protection, specifically the importance of trees. So it made sense to include environmentalist Wangari Maathai into our changemaker lessons. Maathai was a Kenyan biologist who founded the green belt movement in 1977, which has planted over 51 million trees in Kenya (Nobel Prize, n.d.). Her story has many similar characteristics to that of Dr. King: She was put in jail for her work. She didn't carry out her work alone but had many supporters working alongside her. And she received the Nobel Peace Prize (Nobel Prize, n.d.). I sensed that this story would be a useful introduction into the work of the civil rights movement and that my students would draw parallels between Dr. Maathai and Dr. King.

To begin, my colleagues and I developed a set of four questions about what we term *peaceful changemakers*, or people who use nonviolent strategies to bring about big social changes. These questions are:

1. What is the problem?
2. Who is involved?
3. Why is the problem hard to solve?
4. Is it solved? How?

Figure 6.1 illustrates how teachers can use the changemaker chart as a visual aid by recording student comments and ideas about changemakers. Students in K–1 can illustrate their answers to the changemaker questions, while students in grades 2–5 can write sentences and paragraphs in response to the questions.

Changemaker	*What is the problem?*	*Who is involved?*	*Why is it hard to solve the problem?*	*Is it solved? How?*

Figure 6.1: Peaceful changemaker chart.

Visit ***go.SolutionTree.com/diversityandequity*** *for a free reproducible version of this figure.*

When we first developed these questions, we put them in the past tense, but I quickly realized the value of putting them in the present tense. Often, when students learn about the civil rights movement, they consider the struggle for equal rights a problem of the past, and it can be difficult for some to see how inequity is relevant today. This is especially common for White children in privileged institutions. When we frame the question about Dr. King's work in the present tense (What *is* the problem he and many others are trying to solve?), it brings the teaching and the learning into the present as well. It allows the teacher and students to consider ongoing problems of racial injustice. When I introduce Dr. King to my students, I make sure to say, "Today, we are going to learn about a problem that is ongoing and affects all of us—people in the past and people today who work with many others to try and solve it."

I revisit the four questions with students as we learn about various peaceful changemakers throughout the year. Developing common language turns out to be one of the most powerful pieces of the curriculum, as it allows students to examine big social and environmental problems through the lens of simple questions and to return to these questions in upper grades to apply deeper and more complex understandings. For example, in kindergarten, the answer to why problems can be hard to solve is often as simple as, "People didn't listen to their words," or "Some people were violent even when the changemakers were being peaceful." In upper elementary grades, the answers become more complex as students learn some of the systemic barriers that can arise and make social change difficult, such as voter suppression or gerrymandering—the process of redrawing district boundaries to give one political party an advantage over another.

My team and I decided to begin our study of changemakers with a familiar character in one of our favorite picture books to make the learning immediately accessible to the students. Originally, we began this unit by reading *The Lorax* by Dr. Seuss (1971), the story of a creature who tries to prevent the Once-ler from cutting down all the Truffula Trees. Although *The Lorax* gets at the themes of nonviolence, empathy, and courage we wanted to address, there are some problems with *The Lorax,* and with Dr. Seuss himself, that prompted us to change our focus. Researchers Katie Ishizuka and Ramón Stephens (2019) find recurring problems in the way Theodor Geisel (Dr. Seuss) portrayed characters of color in subservient, exotified, and dehumanized roles. Although *The Lorax* wasn't problematic in that way, our team found that it didn't exemplify the values we were hoping to inspire through our changemaker curriculum. The Lorax works alone in his attempts to save the Truffula Trees. There is no collective organizing or movement that supports his work. At the end of the book, he implores the listener to take up his call, to take the last Truffula seed of them all and plant it. We didn't want our students to think that it was up to an individual, whether it be them or the Lorax, to make big, important changes, as this is not how social change works.

As an alternative, we chose *Isabel's House of Butterflies* by Tony Johnston (2005). The book is about a young girl in Michoacán, Mexico, who finds a way to save her favorite tree, a wintering place for thousands of monarch butterflies that migrate from the north. In *Isabel's House of Butterflies,* Isabel works with her mother to make tortillas shaped like butterflies to sell to tourists to make enough money so that they will not have to sell the wood from her favorite tree. The book illustrates how changemaking requires collective action (in this case by Isabel, her parents, and the tourists buying the tortillas). Students immediately related to Isabel, a child their age who felt passionate about something they can relate to: protecting vulnerable creatures.

When I first read this story to my class, we were in the middle of a social studies unit about how trees are important to the environment. We had learned that trees provide so many things we need, including lumber, oxygen, and material for paper. We'd also begun learning about how trees serve as a home for many different creatures. After reading the story, I asked the class to think about the problem that Isabel is trying to solve. They said things like, "She needs to save the tree because it's where the butterflies live" and "Her family doesn't have enough money, so they need to cut down the tree, but Isabel doesn't want them to because then what will happen to the butterflies?" By their response, I could tell they'd understood the concepts I was hoping to convey.

As teachers committed to telling true stories about race and racism, we must actively seek out authors of color and characters of color in our teaching. We must choose stories that align with the goals we set out to accomplish in our curriculum. Social Justice Books (2017), a Teaching for Change project, offers a useful guide for selecting antibias and social justice books for children, young adults, and educators that includes helpful guiding questions, including how many books are by and about people of color and Native Americans. Consider the following suggestions (Social Justice Books, 2017).

- Check the illustrations for stereotypes, tokenism, and invisibility of marginalized identities.
- Consider the message portrayed about lifestyles that differ from the dominant culture.
- Look for changemakers in the story.
- Learn about the author's or illustrator's background.

Thinking critically about the literature you include in your classroom is an essential step in supporting your students to become peaceful changemakers.

While the process for K–2 students is similar for grades 3–5, these older students can delve more deeply into these ideas and have more critical conversations. For example, teachers of older students can illuminate ideas around nonviolence as a strategy for change by teaching about nonviolent direct actions, such as boycotting, marching, and participating in sit-ins.

Classroom Activity

INTRODUCING PEACEFUL CHANGEMAKERS

Introduce the idea of a *peaceful changemaker* as someone who uses peaceful strategies to solve problems. Ask students to think-pair-share about how they solve their own problems peacefully. (Ideas could include, "We use our words, not our bodies. We listen to each other. We ask for help.") Have students share out while you take notes on chart paper. For remote learners, you can use an online tool such as Padlet or Canva. Ask your students to think-pair-share about why being peaceful is important and list these ideas as well. (Ideas could include, "People don't get hurt. We make friendships better again.")

Tell students that starting today, they will begin to learn about people in books and in the world who use peaceful, or nonviolent, strategies to solve big problems that affect everyone. Introduce *Isabel's House of Butterflies* (Johnston, 2005). After reading the book, have students sit around the peaceful changemaker chart in figure 6.1 (page 95), or display the chart on your computer screen for remote learners, and review the story of Isabel using the changemaker chart questions.

Invite students to volunteer to choose specific questions from the chart (What is the problem? Who is involved? Why is it hard to solve? Is it solved?) that they will answer with illustrations. Designate students to assigned tables, or to assigned breakout rooms for remote learners, to draw or write their response. Encourage each table or breakout room to share ideas with one another. Circulate around the room or visit each breakout room, taking dictation when necessary. K–1 students can label their illustrations while you take notes on what they tell you about their drawings; after the lesson, post your notes on the changemaker chart next to their drawings. Students in grades 2–5 can write their responses and add illustrations as well. Ask any students if they would like to share. Repeat this process for other key changemakers you include in your teaching.

Older students can also critically analyze the ways in which famous people they've learned about in the civil rights movement are depicted in textbooks or in the media and what parts of their stories are left out. For example, the common story told about Rosa Parks falsely portrays her as someone who got fed up one day at the injustice of having to give up her seat on the bus for a White person and decided not to get up. In truth, Rosa Parks was a dedicated civil rights activist for two decades prior to the Montgomery bus boycott and continued to organize and protest for several decades after. In 1968, she attended the Black Power convention in Philadelphia, and she considered Malcom X a personal hero (Theoharis, 2021). Ask your older students why they think these parts of her story are frequently left out of the narrative and why it's important to know the whole story.

Peaceful Changemaker Unit: Planting the Seeds of Peace

Review the idea of a peaceful changemaker, or someone who works with others to make big, important changes using peaceful, nonviolent means. Introduce Wangari Maathai, a Kenyan biologist whose organization replants millions of trees in Kenya. Read the book *Wangari's Trees of Peace* by Jeanette Winter (2018).

Ask your students: "How are these problems the same as the problems our other changemakers face? How are they different?" Invite students to volunteer for which part of the changemaker chart they would like to illustrate. Ask students to bring their drawings to the rug (virtual learners can rejoin the main session) and gather everyone around the posted chart. Ask the students designated as sharers to share their illustrations for each part of the chart. Revisit each question on the chart and use call and response to go over the questions again as well as some of the answers that the sharers have drawn or written.

In the following sections, I'll explain how I extended the learning for students, incorporating action projects and using persona dolls to allow students to act out what they were learning. When I felt the students were ready, it was time to revisit Dr. King. Along the way, I realized I needed to communicate with students' families about our conversations about race and racism.

Extending the Learning

Watch a video of Dr. Maathai telling the hummingbird story, the story of a hummingbird who tries to put out a forest fire by carrying single drops of water to the fire (Green Belt Movement, n.d.). In the video, the other animals laugh at the hummingbird and ask her how she thinks she can put out a fire with a single drop of water. She says, "I am doing the best that I can." After the video, ask students what lesson the hummingbird teaches us. Responses could include, "Do your best even when you're small," or "Don't worry if people laugh at you, keep trying." Have the students make their own hummingbirds with two small pom-poms, a toothpick cut in half for the beak, two googly eyes, and two cupcake wrappers. Display these hummingbirds in the classroom underneath a poster that reads "Be

Like the Hummingbird: Do the Best You Can." You can also have your students complete a writing assignment about how they will be like the hummingbird, or what they will choose to focus on in order to do their best. In my class, student responses have included, "I will plant more trees," "I will not argue," and "I will protect the land."

Another way to extend the learning is to read the book *Mama Miti* by Donna Jo Napoli (2010), about the deep wisdom Dr. Maathai had in seeing the importance of each type of tree she replanted. In the book, the refrain "Thaya Nyumba" ("Peace My People") is repeated on almost every page. Ask your students what "Peace My People" meant to Dr. Maathai. Use chart paper, or a virtual bulletin board tool such as Padlet or Canva, to generate a class list. Some items may include trees, food, wood for fire, health, enough money, and so on.

Instruct students to make Thaya Nyumba posters. Give each student a large sheet of construction paper with the phrase Thaya Nyumba and Peace My People typed on the bottom. For virtual learners, create a Padlet with these words included, and ask students to add their images and thoughts. Instruct in-person learners to illustrate the posters with their ideas and ask them to label these drawings. For K–2 students, this is a great activity to do with "buddies" in grades 3–5, who can help younger students understand how peace is related to access. They might mention that having trees close by means people don't have to walk for miles to collect firewood, or allows them to grow their own fruit, makes their life easier, and creates a more peaceful environment. Display the posters in your room with a photo of Wangari Maathai posted nearby.

One last way I extended the learning for my students is by reading the book *A Tree Is Nice* by Janice May Udry (1987). After hearing the story, ask your students to think of what they love about trees and brainstorm some of their ideas. Hand out writing paper with the sentence starter "A tree is nice because . . .", or ask virtual learners to copy down this sentence starter on their own paper, and instruct students to finish the sentence with their idea and draw a picture. Compile these sheets into a class book. Take photos of virtual learners' pages and compile them in an e-reader.

Alternatively, you can have your students make their own small books out of quarter sheets of paper. Instruct them to collect sticks, and bind these books with hole punches, sticks, and rubber bands. Read many books about trees, both fiction and nonfiction, such as *Tree of Life: The Incredible Biodiversity of Life on Earth* by Rochelle Strauss (2013) and *The Spirit of the Baobab Tree* by Dionne Champion and Sherice Grant (2008), to broaden student understanding about the value and importance of trees. Visit mirrorswindowdoors.org (http://mirrorswindowsdoors.org/wp/picture-books-trees-nonfiction) for an extensive list of such books.

Incorporating Action Projects

As I began to introduce peaceful changemakers to my students, I was pleased to see them grappling with the big ideas of courage, justice, and empathy. We decided to choose an action project as a class to practice being changemakers ourselves. We taught our school about the importance of picking up trash around campus so that it didn't make its way into the creek nearby and, eventually, into the ocean.

Students chose people in their own families who work for positive change, and some of these family members came into our classroom to talk to the students about the problems they tried to solve. We dedicated multiple bulletin boards to changemakers and chose characters from books that exemplified the characteristics we decided a person needs to be a changemaker: courage, empathy, and persistence. Each time we studied a changemaker, students chose to illustrate their response to one of our changemaker questions, and I took dictation as they told me their ideas.

I heard things I'd never heard before from my students, things like, "It's hard to solve this problem because people weren't using their listening tool," and "They tried to block her [Wangari Maathai] from doing a good thing [planting trees]." Later, when I asked my students to think about what the changemakers we'd studied so far had in common, including Wangari Maathai, Jane Goodall (the primatologist known for her study and protection of chimpanzees), and Julia Butterfly Hill (who lived in a California redwood tree for over 700 days to prevent clear-cutting), they said things like, "They all make things better for everybody," and "Changemakers solve problems that are big and affect everybody."

Another example of an action project involves including examples of people who work for racial justice. Discussing these individuals is a good opportunity to bring up the Black Lives Matter movement, a movement founded in 2013 in response to the acquittal of Trayvon Martin's murderer (Black Lives Matter, n.d.). The movement's mission is "to eradicate White supremacy and build local power to intervene in violence inflicted on Black communities" (Black Lives Matter, n.d.).

In 2016, as an action project connected to our study of Dr. King and the civil rights movement (influenced by Learning for Justice's [n.d.a] Art and Activism curriculum guide), we worked with our third-grade buddies to make posters that reflected messages of justice we had for our school community and for the world.

These messages were often inspired by Dr. King's principles of nonviolence, which we had also studied that year. They included statements such as, "Love not Hate," "The Universe Is on the Side of Justice," and "Use Kind Words." We hung these posters around the classroom and around the school. I put up my own poster, which read "Black Lives Matter."

This would be the first time I talked about the Black Lives Matter movement with my students, and I felt some familiar fears and concerns: Would my young students be able to grasp the importance of a racial justice movement that centered on the lives of Black and Brown people? Would any of the concerns some of my colleagues and White parents expressed come true in my classroom, namely that this information would divide the students into camps, rather than work to unite them toward a common goal?

Together, we read the poster, and I asked my students to think about the meaning of this message. Jon, a White student, said, "You want us to know that Sasha and Ava's lives matter." Sasha and Ava were the two Black students in the class.

I nodded and said, "That's true. We've learned that there is bias against Black and Brown people through our study of segregated schools and neighborhoods, in seeing there are fewer Black and Brown people in government, and in hearing about Black people being treated unfairly by police. As long as there is bias against Black and Brown people, we have to work against it. That's why we say Black Lives Matter."

Teachers around the United States teach about Black Lives Matter. The Black Lives Matter at School movement first started in Seattle in 2016 and has evolved into an action that lasts a week each year and occurs in schools across the country. Visit www.blacklivesmatteratschool.com/resources.html for curriculum resources, guiding principles, and a starter kit. Additionally, the National Education Association's (n.d.) EdJustice has many resources for teaching about Black Lives Matter and race and racism generally.

Using Persona Dolls

Our class explored these new concepts around changemaking and what it requires in the months of November and December. As January neared, I felt some familiar fears around how I would approach the problem of racism with my students, though I was determined to say things I hadn't said before, to sit with my own discomfort, and to allow conversations to happen.

I thought about how disturbed I'd been by White students singling out Black students during previous class conversations about Dr. King and wondered if this would lessen if I introduced ideas around exclusion based on differences *prior* to talking about Dr. King. To begin, I decided to use our class puppets to act out scenarios of exclusion based on differences. In my classroom, our puppets serve as persona dolls—classroom dolls whose name, birth date, family, likes, dislikes, and so on remain as constant as those characteristics do for real children in the classroom. I often use persona dolls as the vehicle for discussing social-emotional issues that come up in the room and problems that need solving on the playground. We also use our puppets to teach specific social-emotional skills, such as courage and empathy.

The puppets are well loved by kindergarteners, many of whom are at the age where they easily enter into the magical world of make believe, while still mostly understanding the difference between reality and imagination.

When two zebra puppets shared that the lion puppet couldn't play with them because she wasn't a zebra, my students were immediately outraged. "That's not fair," they told the zebras. "You can't say you can't play. It doesn't matter if she's not a zebra. Use your empathy tool." The students were pleased when the zebras approached the lion to apologize and invite her to play. Afterward, we discussed the dangers of excluding others based on differences and the importance of inclusion. I repeated this with other puppets; the cat puppets wouldn't let the dogs join their game, and the sloths wouldn't let the lamb have tea with them. I was pleased with all the reasons my students gave for inclusion, such as "Everyone gets to be happy" and "No one should be alone if they don't want to be."

Revisiting Dr. King

Finally, it was time to learn about Dr. King. I picked up the same book I'd read before, *Happy Birthday, Martin Luther King* (Marzollo, 2006), though I prefaced it by saying we were going to learn about another changemaker who worked to solve a big social problem. The students then had a context for the story and the context of changemaking, and the feeling in the room was one of curiosity and receptiveness, as is the general atmosphere around the conversation of changemakers in kindergarten.

In the introduction to her book, Jean Marzollo (2006) suggests that the assassination may be too difficult for elementary students to hear and advises skipping over it if necessary. At the time, I didn't have a replacement story that I felt would be more appropriate for this age, and I didn't feel great about skipping this section of the story. It reminded me of how I had rushed through parts of the book, skipped pages, or stopped conversations midstream.

Determined not to make mistakes of the past, I read each page of Jean Marzollo's (2006) book, including the page that references Dr. King's murder. When one of my students said, "I know what happened to him, he was shot!" I responded by saying, "We are going to focus on his life in this class, as well as many other people who worked alongside him." I had photos of some of the people I'd learned about that summer, and I displayed them for the students. I introduced Claudette Colvin, a Black teenager who refused to get up from her seat on the bus for a White passenger. I showed a picture of James Reeb, a White minister who traveled to Selma for the Selma to Montgomery March. I told them about Ruby Bridges, a Black first grader who was the first to integrate an elementary school in the South. I asked my students what they noticed about these changemakers. "They are all different," one student offered. "One is six years old," another said. "They are all changemakers," said a third.

I put up a more recent photo of Ruby Bridges as an adult and told the students that she is still alive, and continues her work as a civil rights activist, author, and speaker. In future lessons, I would read the book *The Story of Ruby Bridges* by Robert Coles (2010) and have deeper discussions about the courage it took for Ruby Bridges, who was the same age at the time as many of my students, to enter a school building when so many people did not want her there, and the impact her courage had. But with this first introduction, I wanted my students to know, by seeing that Ruby Bridges was still alive and working, that the civil rights movement was not in the distant past, and that not all changemakers die in the process of making change. "That's her *now?*" one student asked, coming closer to the board where I'd posted the photos of her as a child and an adult side by side.

After I finished reading *Happy Birthday, Martin Luther King* (Marzollo, 2006), one of my White students raised his hand and said, "My mom would have had to sit on the back of the bus. She's Black." I knew this student's mother and knew that she wasn't Black. He went on to say, "She's darker than me. She wouldn't have been allowed to sit on the front of the bus."

I realized the student was describing his mother's skin tone, she was slightly tan, and that he had no idea what the terms *Black* and *White* meant. I noticed some students studying their own skin and wondered how many of them had an understanding of race at all, or even skin color.

Another student said, "This is a lot like Wangari! She went to jail, too, just like Martin Luther King Jr."

And another student said, "Just because you're police, it doesn't make you right. Wangari was right because she was helping the women and the trees." Some others nodded.

Then, one of my White students raised her hand to say, "Tara's brown, and she wouldn't be able to be at this school."

I glanced at Tara, who sat quietly. Other students turned to look at her.

Again, I wasn't sure how to bring Tara's voice in the room, and how to keep my White students from singling out Black students. I was also disturbed that this was the first time that skin color had seemed important in a conversation, in the context of racism, as if Tara having brown skin only mattered when we learned about racism. I was equally disturbed about a lack of foundational understanding about skin color and race for many of my students.

I said, "Yes, and, as a White person, I would have been able to sit where I wanted."

I paused, feeling incredibly uncomfortable at having named my race in front of my students. It was the first time I'd done that.

My students looked at me, waiting. "Does that seem fair?" I asked them.

They shook their heads, and a couple of students called out, "No!"

"What's unfair about it?" I asked.

"Everyone should be able to sit where they want to sit," a student offered.

"You can't say someone can't sit somewhere because of how they look," another student said.

"I agree with you," I said, closing the book, and holding onto it with both hands.

"That's why we all have to work hard to make sure things like this don't happen."

This lesson did not feel done, but I wasn't sure what else to add.

Another book to introduce Dr. King's life to students is *The Story of Martin Luther King Jr.* by Johnny Ray Moore (2015). This is a board book appropriate for kindergarteners, as it focuses on Dr. King's life as a young child. The book points out the injustices he observed around him and how these influenced his desire to work for fairness and justice.

Even though the book doesn't mention the assassination, inevitably, a student often brings it up, and others want to know the details. While I don't go into detail, I also don't deny the truth. I acknowledge that this happened by simply saying, "Yes, he was killed. In this class, we are going to focus on his life and the work he and many others did and continue to do."

If a student wants to know or say more about the assassination, we have a one-on-one conversation later so they can share their comments and questions, and I can validate their knowledge or acknowledge their curiosity. I advise them to ask their questions and continue these discussions at home, as in the kindergarten classroom we are not going to talk in detail about Dr. King's assassination.

I also make sure to tell my students that the fact that Dr. King was killed is why it takes courage to be a changemaker. I let them know it's not easy to work for change when people don't agree with you and aren't peaceful themselves, but that there are always many people who do agree and support movements for change and justice.

It is important to note that I discovered *The Story of Martin Luther King Jr.* by Johnny Ray Moore (2015) when I reached out to the Black families in my classroom and asked them if they had any favorite books on the topic at home.

Sending a Letter Home to Families

The following year, in 2013, I fully accepted that not knowing what my students already knew or didn't know about Dr. King, and what their families wanted them to know, was negatively impacting my teaching and my students' experience. I reached out to the Black families in my class first, as these were the voices that had been most silent in class discussions and the voices I wanted to include. Now, I send a letter home to every family in my class about a month before beginning instruction about Dr. King. See figure 6.2 for a sample of the letter I send home to families.

Each year, after sending out this letter, I receive responses from families that impact the way I begin the conversation about Dr. King and the civil rights movement. Having data about whether students talk about these topics at home has allowed me to gain a more accurate sense of where and how to begin. It allows me to know which students may need more guidance and which students may benefit from one-on-one talks with me to share their knowledge or ask questions. This communication home also allows parents and caregivers to ask their questions about the topic before I begin teaching about it, which can circumvent potential problems later on. I've come to view the letter home as an essential piece of the instruction, as it works to build trust among families and eliminates any guesswork I might be tempted to do about what my students do and don't know.

Dear Kindergarten Families,

Our study of peaceful changemakers in kindergarten involves learning about and celebrating the themes of justice and peaceful change. We will be reading books about famous, and not so famous, people who have peacefully worked to bring about positive change in their communities and around the world, and have created a changemaker chart in our classroom. Soon, we will begin talking about Martin Luther King Jr. as someone who worked alongside others, through nonviolent means, to change unfair laws and make our country a more inclusive and just place.

Before we begin this study, we would like to know how you approach this topic with your child at home. What does your child know about Martin Luther King Jr. already, or will this be the first time hearing his story? Are there any themes or ideas that you stress, any parts of his life story that you do not share (such as how he died), or any parts of his life that you emphasize? Your feedback will help inform our discussions in the classroom.

Thank you!

Your Kindergarten Teachers

Figure 6.2: Sample letter sent home to families.

A Work in Progress

Back in the classroom in 2013, I'd made progress in teaching the big ideas around changemaking, and my students were starting to grapple with themes of fairness, nonviolence, and what it takes to make big social changes. However, I hadn't succeeded in having an inclusive conversation about Dr. King, where White students didn't single out Black students, and where White students wouldn't do all the talking. I'd used our class puppets to act out scenarios of exclusion based on difference, and we'd talked about the feelings that arise from this type of exclusion and why it's important not to engage in it. But we hadn't yet talked openly about racism. My students needed support in understanding what race meant. The next step was to open up a deeper conversation about race and racism with my students.

CHAPTER 7

A DEEPER CONVERSATION ABOUT RACE

How could I get to the root of the challenge I was facing with my students around race and racism? I found helpful guidance through the lens of antiracism. In his book, *How to Be an Antiracist,* Kendi (2019) defines *racism* as "a marriage of racist policies and racist ideas that produces and normalizes racial inequities" (pp. 17–18). Considering Kendi's definitions of racism and antiracism helps to frame the problem I was observing in my classroom in terms of racial equity. If racism is about policies and ideas that produce and normalize racial inequities, then becoming an antiracist teacher would necessarily require me to teach strategies and ideas that would result in a more equal footing.

In the context of our classroom conversations, this meant all voices would be included in every conversation, and especially the conversation about racism. If White voices ruled the conversation in my classroom, my teaching itself was perpetuating existing inequities. Finding a way to invite and include the voices of students of color would disrupt this pattern, and I hoped it would achieve greater equity. I had to find an antiracist way of teaching about racism.

In this chapter, I detail how I continued to develop our changemaker curriculum to talk explicitly about race and racism. I started by laying foundational knowledge about skin color before explaining why stereotyping based on skin color is dangerous. Next, I talked to students about bias against the color brown and the differences between skin color and race. One of the most important lessons happened when we learned that we are all similar and different, which is something to celebrate. With these concepts in place, students were finally ready to learn about the problem of racism.

Foundational Knowledge About Skin Color and Race

There was clearly a gap in my young students' knowledge: many of them did not know anything about skin color, let alone race. I assumed this was because my White students hadn't had any conversations at home about race or skin color. Later, when I interviewed White parents of first- and second-grade White students at my school, I learned that many of them were waiting for their child to ask a question or to reach the "right" age before they said anything about race.

I also sensed that parents of color were having conversations about race and skin color at home more frequently. I based this on the way parents of color responded to a survey I'd sent out, informal conversations we'd had, and my own experience as a White mother of Black girls. I made sure my girls had books, toys, and role models that reflected their racial identity, and I sought spaces and places where they weren't in the minority. I had to be intentional about that. I had to confront the inequities we faced and work against them by seeking out role models and play materials that affirmed their racial identity.

Yes, my students demonstrated that they could grasp big, important concepts around social justice, but the tenor and tone of the conversation about race and racism had stayed the same year after year: students were confused, made misinformed statements, and singled out students of color. I needed to provide foundational understandings before we talked about racism in order to clear up the confusion, answer questions, and provide correct information.

One afternoon, during free play, I watched a small group of students in the corner of the room building an elaborate castle out of blocks. One of the students, Chris, dumped a plastic bin of multicolored bears onto the floor next to the castle and picked through them, carefully pulling out all the blue bears and standing them up in a circle around the castle. He was talking quietly as he set up the bears, and I moved closer to hear. "Only the blue bears can guard the castle," Chris told the group, pushing the yellow and red bears out of the way. Another student, Thomas, held a yellow bear in his hand as he watched his classmate lining up all the blue bears. I sat down next to them. "What is it about the blue bears that makes them the only ones who can guard?" I asked, genuinely curious. Knowing blue was Chris's favorite color, I expected to hear, "Because they are blue!" Chris looked at me, then at the yellow bear in Thomas's hand. "I don't know," he said, shrugging. "Yellow bears can be strong!" Thomas offered, placing a yellow bear next to one of the blue bears. Chris paused, and then reached for a handful of red and yellow bears from the castle. "All the bears can guard the castle!" he pronounced, moving some of the blue bears out of the way to make room for the red and yellow ones.

Conversations like these created opportunities to take our learning about skin color into discussions of race, racism, stereotyping, and bias, and they prompted lessons and read-alouds where we could talk explicitly about the dangers of stereotyping based on skin color.

We read *The Skin You Live In* by Michael Tyler (2005), a poetic and beautifully illustrated book about what skin is and what skin isn't—that skin color does not mean bad, good, smart, or dumb. We also read *Skin Again* by bell hooks (2017), which reinforces the idea that you have to go deeper than skin color to get to know someone.

Explore Where Skin Color Comes From

I decided to spend the first few months of school simply reading, teaching about, and discussing skin color. I read several books that explored the diversity of skin tones, including *The Colors of Us* by Karen Katz (2002), *All the Colors of the Earth* by Sheila Hamanaka (1999), and *Shades of People* by Shelley Rotner and Sheila M. Kelly (2010).

I also brought in texts that described, in simple, scientific terms, where skin color comes from and what accounts for darker or lighter skin.

One of the most effective books I've found for this discussion is *All the Colors We Are* by Katie Kissinger (2014), which uses simple terms to explain the three factors that contribute to skin color: the sun, where your ancestors are from, and melanin. In the beginning, the book asks students where they think their skin color comes from. Here are some of the explanations my students gave:

- "It just comes from your mom. Your dad has nothing to do with it."
- "Your skin gets cooked inside. That's why it's darker."
- "You just have it. Nobody gives it to you."

These responses confirmed my suspicion that I needed to clear up the confusion around skin color. After we read the book several times and I explained terms many of my students were unfamiliar with (such as *ancestors* and *melanin*), my students were able to give the facts about where skin color comes from. Knowledge finally took the place of their misinformed or biased ideas.

Discover Accurate Colors

This was a great start, but I wanted the learning to go deeper than sitting and listening. I wanted my students to actively engage with the learning, as this is how young students learn most effectively. I brought in paint chips for students to compare to their skin and come up with poetic names to describe their skin tones. To adapt this lesson for virtual learners, display paint chips on the screen and ask students to find any items around their house that match the colors. In the classroom, students mixed paint to find our skin tones. We talked about how no one is white or black like construction paper, and how we are all different shades of brown. I bought many shades of skin color pencils, crayons, and markers. I also made sure students were adding skin color to the White students in their drawings and stories, not only to the students of color; I wanted them to know that we all have a race and being White is not equated with "normal." My students became fascinated with each other's skin colors and loved choosing the pencil or marker that was just right for their illustrations.

Discuss Skin Color

Another challenge I faced was that some of my White students tended to see the students of color in the room as somehow the same. Leo, one of my White students, always asked his White classmates which color pencil best aligned with their skin tone. One day I watched him drawing a picture of a Black student in the room; he picked a pencil without asking his classmate if this was the right color to use for his skin. I stopped him and said, "How do you know that's the right skin color for Jeremy?" He looked up at me and said, "Jeremy and Nick are the same—they're both chestnut." I asked, "How do you know that?" He paused, looked over at Jeremy, and said, "Jeremy, is chestnut the right color for you?" Jeremy immediately replied, "My skin is mahogany." Leo put down his pencil and found the mahogany skin tone pencil. This represented an important shift in Leo's understanding of skin color and race. Rather than assuming about a student of color in the room, he was learning to stop and ask questions. The open dialogue about skin color also allowed me to see students' tendency to classify and categorize, challenge their thinking, and teach them skills to communicate with respect around their differences.

Bias Against Brown

Another one of my goals was to address biases against brown. Over the years, I'd heard young White students make disparaging comments about brown as a color.

I'd also heard from preschool teachers about times when a White student said to a child of color, "Your skin is dirty" or "Your skin is like poop." First-grade teachers have shared times a White child has said to a Black child, "I don't like your skin color."

Brown, as a color, is not often celebrated in poems and songs made readily available to early childhood educators. While there are many poems and songs that celebrate each color of the rainbow, brown is often omitted. In fact, some children's songs I came across actively disparaged the color brown. I searched for a way to address the bias behind these comments.

A colleague recommended a book of poetry, *Tan to Tamarind,* by Malathi Michelle Iyengar (2009), that celebrates brown in nature, skin tones, food, and experiences. Following the author's curriculum guide, after reading the poems to my students, I brought in various brown spices and food—such as cloves, coffee grounds, cinnamon, and cocoa powder—and instructed my students to touch, smell, and describe them. We made a list of all the descriptive words we could think of like *strong*, *sweet*, and *spicy*, and used these words to write poems about brown. We also used the spices to create artwork, and I hung their art around the room alongside their poems. I made a point to include brown in any discussion of favorite colors, informally and during lessons, such as during our unit on poetry. Here's a list I've compiled of books that celebrate the color brown.

- *Big Hair, Don't Care* by Crystal Swain-Bates (2013)
- *Brown Boy Joy* by Thomishia Booker (2018)
- *Brown Like Me* by Noelle Lamperti (2000)
- *Crown: An Ode to the Fresh Cut* by Derrick Barnes (2017)
- *Hair Dance!* by Dinah Johnson (2007)
- *I Am Enough* by Grace Byers (2018)
- *I Am Perfectly Designed* by Karamo Brown (2019)
- *I Love My Hair!* by Natasha Anastasia Tarpley (2001)
- *Pretty Brown Face* by Andrea and Brian Pinkney (1997)
- *Shades of Black: A Celebration of Our Children* by Sandra L. Pinkney (2006)
- *Sulwe* by Lupita Nyong'o (2019)
- *Tan to Tamarind: Poems About the Color Brown* by Malathi Michelle Iyengar (2009)

Before long, I noticed the biased statements about the color brown fading from the classroom. White students no longer assumed that students of color were related to one another. No one thought a Black adult who entered the room automatically belonged with a Black student. Now that students had a safe and compassionate space to examine and challenge these assumptions, their tendency to put like with like, and their aversion to brown, they were able to learn the truth. They gained the skills they needed to appreciate and understand skin color.

The Difference Between Skin Color and Race

One of the most challenging aspects of this teaching is pulling apart the difference between skin color and race in a way that young children will understand. The teaching I've covered in this chapter so far is essential for giving students a foundational understanding about skin color, as well as interrupting any forming biases. But it doesn't address race as a concept. Race is a much more complicated and confusing concept, one that many adults have a hard time grasping and talking about with any consensus.

Before I was ready to talk with students about race, I needed to understand some fundamental things about my own racial identity. Through reading books like *Witnessing Whiteness* by Shelly Tochluk (2010) and *White Like Me* by Tim Wise (2011), I became more and more aware of the privilege associated with white skin. I saw this as I studied the history of Whiteness (page 43) and observed everyday examples in my own life—such as never having to be a spokesperson for an entire race of people, never being questioned by an authority figure (such as a police officer) because of the color of my skin, and always seeing myself represented in media. But how was I going to explain this to my students? None of us are white or black like construction paper, and yet these categories do exist. We need to understand them and how they operate in our society to work against racism. How could I express that to young students?

To begin, I decided to talk about my own race in front of my students, to explain the difference between my skin color and my race. I gathered my students on our reading rug and brought a piece of white construction paper with me, along with a paint chip I'd used in a lesson where we'd come up with poetic names for our skin tones. "Remember how we learned that I'm not white like paper?" I asked my students, holding up the white paper against my arm to demonstrate. The class nodded. I held up the paint chip and compared it to my skin. "I learned that my skin is similar to this paint chip, desert tan," I reminded the class. "We learned that we all have skin color and that we are different shades. We know that skin color comes from the sun, how much melanin we have, and where our ancestors are from. Today we are going to talk about the difference between skin color and race," I said. "My skin color is tan, and even though my skin color isn't white like paper, my race is White." I paused, taking a breath.

"The terms *White* and *Black* refer to how people identify as a group to categories, rather than to colors." I could see telltale signs that I was losing some of my students: students crinkled their eyebrows, looked around the room, or played with the frayed edges of our rug. "We need to know these categories in order to understand how they've been used to leave some people out, and to include others." I reached for the book I'd also brought to the rug, Julius Lester's (2005) *Let's Talk About Race,* and motioned for my students to move closer so they could see the book.

I read the book without further explanation. *Let's Talk About Race* emphasizes how we all have stories inside us, such as our favorite things to do, or eat, or drink, or when and where we were born. To introduce race, Lester (2005) writes that race is a part of our story and, just like we have stories about ourselves, each race has a story about itself. Lester (2005) writes, "and that story is almost always the same: 'my race is better than your race.' Some stories are true. Some are not. Those who say, 'my race is better than your race' are telling a story that is not true" (p. 16). The book also emphasizes getting to know someone before making any assumptions about them, a theme we had been stressing all year. I ended the lesson that day hoping that this first introduction to race would help lay the foundation for future lessons about racism and White supremacy, knowing that I had just scratched the surface on this complex topic.

During this time, our classroom adopted a refrain that has become a foundational part of my work. I read the picture book *Same, Same but Different,* by Jenny Sue Kostecki-Shaw (2011), about two boys who live in different cities and countries and become pen pals. My students loved this book, and they often pulled it off the shelf for me to read or flipped through the pages during free time. I noticed them using the refrain "same, same but different" during other times of the day: in the middle of a mathematics lesson, or after listening to a story, or when talking among themselves about their own similarities and differences. I noticed that this language was helping them to compare and categorize without singling out others and to draw parallels and make connections across disciplines.

As my students' curiosity and excitement about "same, same but different" grew, this exploration of similarities and differences expanded beyond skin color differences and into family structures, hair texture and styles, and open conversations about gender. During read-alouds and class discussions, my students began asking questions about what makes a family a family, how you can tell if someone is a boy or a girl, why people dress differently in different parts of the world, and so on. In response, the kindergarten teaching team established a unit on families. We included books that represented a variety of family structures, such as *My Family, Your Family* by Lisa Bullard (2015), *Two Homes* by Claire Masurel (2003), and *And Tango Makes Three* by Justin Richardson and Peter Parnell (2015). We learned about each of the families in the classroom, made class books about what each student likes to do with their family, counted and graphed the number of people in our families, and created anchor charts like "What Makes a Family a Family?" Each year, my students come to the consensus that the one thing all families share is love.

To encourage my students to be curious and ask questions about the differences around them, rather than make assumptions or pass judgments, I began to use Bishop's (1990) frame of windows and mirrors, an approach to teaching and to diversifying children's literature I've discussed in previous chapters. As we talked about similarities, I asked my students to think of looking in a mirror and seeing their reflection. When they were learning about something different from them, I asked them to think about looking out a window and feeling curious about what they saw. This frame allows students to think of differences as places to ask questions, to be curious and open, rather than be dismissive or immediately judgmental. This was yet another way to reinforce the importance of thinking critically about assumptions, as well as recognizing commonalities with others.

As I've taught this content over the years, I've observed students becoming more open, more curious, and more skilled at articulating sophisticated questions and understandings about how diverse people are alike and different.

A Celebration of Differences

Before adopting antiracist teaching, I feared that talking about differences would cause my students to separate by these differences—I thought they'd sort one another into categories and be less united as a community. But rather than creating divisions among students, I found the open conversations about differences and the airing of misconceptions created *greater unity* among my students. No camps have formed. I've never yet witnessed my students separating themselves into groups based on shared traits.

This concern about division is an error that many White parents and educators share. I now see this idea of not needing to discuss racial differences as an aspect of White privilege. By contrast, my personal research has shown that many parents and educators of color do not share this privilege; they address racial difference with students in order to prepare them to deal with and manage bias and racism.

Elsewhere in the book, I've demonstrated how students frequently commented on their differences and singled out students of color before adopting the change-maker curriculum and antiracist practices. Through our continued discussion and emphasis on how we are all the same and different from one another in many ways, students understood it was no longer appropriate to form camps based on observed similarities. So, while we may share a similar hair color to one friend, we also may have different interests, or different family structures, or a different shade of skin. While we may have different skin from a friend, we may share other similarities, such as similar interests. These lessons must go hand in hand so that young children get the message that we are all different *and* the same.

Table 7.1 summarizes key antiracist practices teachers can incorporate in the classroom and examples of actions or phrases they can use.

TABLE 7.1: Key Antiracist Elements in the Classroom

Key Antiracist Element	Example of Teacher Action or Dialogue
Speak honestly and openly about bias, what it is, and how to prevent it from forming.	"You may think you know something about someone by looking at them, but you actually don't. When you make an assumption about someone, especially someone who is different from you, that assumption is biased or unfair. The only way to know anything about anyone is to get to know them, to know their story."
Respond to moments of bias and prejudice in the moments they occur.	"What you said was an example of bias. Remember, in this classroom we work to fight against bias and prejudice whenever they happen. What can we do to make it better?"

continued →

Teach children how to check their assumptions and learn to ask questions instead.	When you hear a student assume someone's race, gender, religion, or anything about someone who is different from them, remind them that they can't tell by looking. When you hear a student make an assumption based on an observed difference, teach them how to ask a question instead. Use "I wonder" as a sentence starter when you model asking questions, and do research together, as a class, to find out what these differences actually mean.
Speak openly and honestly about White supremacy and how it functioned and continues to function in our society.	"One of the beliefs that our country was founded on was the false idea that some people were better than others because of the color of their skin. When we say White supremacy, we are talking about an unfair system that is as old as our country, that gives privileges and rights to White people and not to people of color." If you teach in a predominately White community, ask your students to think about why their school and their neighborhood look the way they do. Help them draw connections between unfair systems, such as redlining and other forms of housing discrimination, and the racial demographics of their community. This will help your students begin to understand the legacy and impact of systemic racism.

An Evolution of My Teaching Practices

As January 2014 neared, I wondered whether our learning of similarities and differences might prevent White students from singling out Black students in the room when it came time to talk about racism. Would the antiracist practices I'd adopted during the previous months change our conversation about Dr. King in any significant way?

When I sat down in front of the class to read about Dr. King, I explained, as I'd done the year before, that we were going to learn about another important change-maker who worked to solve a big problem that affects all of us. "The problem we are going to learn about today, and for the next several weeks, is called racism."

I held up the book *Let's Talk About Race* (Lester, 2005). I said, "For a long time, and in some places still today, there was a story that was not a true story, and it was a dangerous story. That story said that White was better than other races." (Today I also define this as White supremacy, though, at the time, I hadn't started using that language with my students.) "This is a big problem because it means that people who aren't considered White have been treated unfairly and haven't had the same opportunities as White people."

I put down *Let's Talk About Race* and held up the board book *The Story of Martin Luther King Jr.* by Johnny Ray Moore (2015). Earlier in the year, I'd sent home a letter asking families what their children knew or didn't know about Dr. King and what parents and caregivers hoped their children would learn.

Jessica, whose family had recommended the book to me, jumped up from her place on the carpet. "That's my favorite bedtime story!" she exclaimed, immediately coming to the front of the room to share what she knew about the story. This was the first time in all the years I'd been teaching that a student of color's voice was the first one present in the conversation about Dr. King. The energy in the room was very different from what it had been in the past. Jessica's classmates were eager to hear their friend's favorite bedtime story read aloud.

After listening to the story, without interruption, my students stayed focused on the injustice of the problems Dr. King was trying to solve. I circled among the students, observing them as they illustrated their answers to the changemaker question of their choice (page 95). They were talking about the ideas I'd been hoping to hear them grapple with and discuss: why it's unfair to exclude another based on difference, how Dr. King had to have courage, what they would have done had they been there.

The next day, I read two books: *A Sweet Smell of Roses* by Angela Johnson (2007) and *The Story of Ruby Bridges* by Robert Coles (2010). *A Sweet Smell of Roses* is about two children who sneak away from home to join a march led by Dr. King. *The Story of Ruby Bridges* is the true story of the first child to integrate an elementary school in the South. Midway through *The Story of Ruby Bridges*, an illustration shows Ruby entering her new school building surrounded by angry White people, their mouths open, fingers pointing at her. An Asian student, Sean, called out, "I don't like how the White people are acting in this story." I saw some heads nodding around the room. I lowered the book and nodded along with them. "Neither do I," I said. "Ruby Bridges must have been scared," I added. A student in the back of the room, Sophia, added, "She had to use her courage tool!"

After reading the story, as I'd done the year before, I held up a photo of Ruby Bridges as an adult, to show that she was still alive and working for justice. I also showed them pictures of people of all races who were active in the civil rights movement. I held up a photo of James Reeb, the White minister who was also a civil rights activist, and said, "There are people of all races who work to make things better and fairer, who agree that Ruby Bridges and all children should be able to go to any school." I wanted my students to understand the diversity of people involved in solving the problem, while also not diminishing their growing awareness of the danger of White supremacy and White supremacists.

I asked the class to think again about who is involved in the problem Dr. King was trying to solve. I stopped at a table where two students were drawing their response to my question. One dumped all the skin color markers onto the table, all different shades of brown, and said, "These are all the people who marched with Martin Luther King Jr." He then lined the markers up in a row, mixing the colors together, and said, "They were all different shades." The other student had been watching him, and she leaned over and began taking the tops off the markers and creating her own line of marker tops. "And these are all the kids!" she said. "Who also marched with Dr. King and had to solve the problem!"

After the students left that day, I felt energized and excited to return to this topic the following day. I no longer felt deeply disappointed in myself; I didn't dread trying again. That's when I knew something big had shifted in my teaching and in my students' learning. No one had singled anyone out in the conversation. I didn't have to clear up any confusion about what skin color is or isn't, who in the story is Black or White, or what that meant for my students. It felt like they were prepared and ready to have a conversation about racism. They'd had ample time to examine what it means to be similar and different in terms of skin color, hair, family structure, and gender. And we'd been exploring how to use nonviolent strategies to solve big social problems. I had finally found a way to communicate the themes I most care about as an educator, and my students were ready to think about them. As a result, we had broken a toxic silence.

CHAPTER 8

PARENTS AND CAREGIVERS PARTNER IN THE CONVERSATION

There's no question that parent engagement is a cornerstone of creating a positive classroom environment and supporting student achievement. But it's also an essential component for teachers committed to adopting antiracist practices in the classroom. In 2021, parents protested teaching about race and racism in their children's schools (Zou, 2021). While the dynamics that gave rise to these protests are beyond the scope of this book, parental response to antiracist teaching in the classroom is relevant to the work we're discussing here. The backlash seen during 2021 tells us that parents and caregivers want to be involved in students' learning about race and racism, and teachers have a responsibility to give them the opportunity to do so. In fact, the success of antiracist education will likely depend on a teacher's willingness and ability to engage parents in the process.

There are many steps teachers can take to engage families when discussing race and racism, and many ways they can go about it. Regardless of the approach, though, the foundation of these efforts should be one of trust, mutual respect, and understanding. As teachers, we know that it's best to be proactive rather than reactive in building connections with families.

In this chapter, we'll explore how to create effective family engagement practices by making them accessible, equitable, and collaborative. The reality is that parents and caregivers are learning right alongside teachers and students. If teachers take a proactive stance, inviting families into the conversation from the beginning, they can avoid potential conflict and maximize learning for all involved. Ultimately, when teachers are willing to have conversations with and learn from families, they find that their insight, resources, and questions benefit the classroom conversations around race and racism.

Effective Family Engagement Practices

It's important to remember that family engagement practices do not automatically establish the kind of trust necessary for all families to feel included in a classroom or in a school community. For example, a working parent doesn't have the same access to volunteer during a school field trip as a stay-at-home parent does. Similarly, back-to-school events and other evening school gatherings may not be accessible to parents and caregivers without childcare. Adjusting these events to ensure equity and accessibility whenever possible is an important step in bonding with families. Successful family engagement practices must be intentional, thoughtful, equitable, and accessible for all families.

In my school, for many years our back-to-school nights were adult-only gatherings, which meant that any parents or caregivers who didn't have another adult on hand to babysit weren't able to attend. Now, our back-to-school nights include a free childcare option so that it is more widely accessible. We also have evening dialogues with families and morning coffee meetings where we engage in parent education topics or curriculum-sharing activities. Offering multiple meeting times ensures that more people can attend, which has resulted in greater parent participation throughout the year.

As you consider the following sections, think about what changes you could make to your parent engagement efforts to make them more accessible and equitable. How might this change the connections you're able to create with families at your school?

A Welcoming Atmosphere

Changing systems can be difficult, especially in institutions where these systems have been in place for a long time. I once attended a parent meeting about a fundraising event and immediately noticed the lack of diversity at this meeting. That was true of many of the committees and parent gatherings at the time—most of the attendees were White stay-at-home moms. When I brought this up, one parent said that the invitation to come to the meeting was open to any parent or caregiver at the school. He thought that by inviting everyone, the meeting was necessarily inclusive. However, that perspective only sees the responsibility of the parent to make arrangements to attend; it doesn't see the meeting's structural responsibility to consider the diverse needs and privileges of parents.

Too often, diversity and inclusion initiatives stop at the invitation level. The invitations or applications themselves aren't intentionally exclusive, yet the schools or committees or events aren't diverse. There are many reasons for this, including the affordability of independent schools, the structures around when committee meetings and events happen, and the history of a school community or committee. Creating truly inclusive systems requires shifting priorities and making structural changes with accessibility and equity in mind. Diversity consultant Steven Jones (2020) puts it this way: In order to create a truly inclusive environment, it's not enough to invite people into the institution, you have to create an environment where "diversity of thought is the currency for inclusion . . . where bringing up differences is a low risk proposition" (Jones, 2020).

If you want to create a family engagement system that results in greater diversity, attendance, and participation, everyone must feel that you value their ideas, that you want their input, and that they belong. That means listening to what students and families need and accommodating those needs. Listen especially to students and families traditionally underrepresented in schools, school boards, and PTAs. Early on his twenty-three-year career as head of Lick-Wilmerding High School, an independent high school in San Francisco, Al Adams sensed that his school was "playing happy family." Students of color at his school were not feeling as welcomed or included as White students, especially White students who had grown up in independent schools. He asked, *Who feels at home when they walk in the door?* To find out, he asked the students of color to talk candidly about their experiences at the school, and their responses led to what he calls "institutional soul searching" (Adams, 2014, p. 43), a process every public and private institution can undertake.

This soul searching resulted in important structural changes: the school included student expenses like books and lunch programs in tuition, provided funding for extra expenses like dances and school trips, developed a Student Strategies Center to help students succeed academically, and committed to equity pedagogy (a process of deeply knowing each student and what they needed to succeed). These changes built a culture in which all students and families felt fully welcome and were encouraged to bring their whole, authentic selves to the community. The school made it a priority to ensure that each child and family felt cared for, cared about, and celebrated.

A Collaborative Process, Not a Tool

Family engagement specialist Allyson Criner Brown (2019) writes about how she learned the difference between engaging with families as a classroom management tool and as a collaborative process. While her intentions were good, and the positive interactions with families had a positive impact on students, she was using her family engagement as a kind of classroom management tool, a system of what she calls "carrots and sticks" (Brown, 2019, p. 121). The problem with this approach is that it was one-directional. Her goal was to make things run more smoothly in the classroom rather than to collaborate with families, inviting them to teach her about students and what they needed to succeed in her classroom.

Brown (2019) offers several strategies for effective family engagement.

- Value parent perspectives by collecting feedback.
- Share feedback with administration when necessary.
- Establish school-based parent centers for Black families to share about their experiences and support one another.

She writes, "Schools need black families at the table to meet the social, emotional, and academic needs of black students" (Brown, 2019, p. 126).

Brown (2019) serves as executive director of Teaching for Change, an organization dedicated to building social justice in the classroom. Teaching for Change's (n.d.) parent engagement model seeks to overcome boundaries between parents, teaching, schools, and communities. Their approach, the Tellin' Stories Approach, "is based on the concepts of racial equity, popular education, community organization, and research on family engagement" (Teaching for Change, n.d.). Researchers Anne Henderson and Karen Mapp (2002) examined fifty-one research studies for evidence that family and community connections with schools make a difference in student success. They find real gains for students depended on the following criteria: well-designed and proactive strategies to engage families; innovative family engagement practices that build close collaboration between parents and educators; and meaningful meetings, conferences, and communications (Henderson & Mapp, 2002). In response to more recent studies that claim parent involvement is overrated, researchers Mapp, Henderson, and Hill (2014) assert that real gains can be made for students when parent involvement strategies are strategically designed to meet the needs of families. The researchers suggest the following strategies to ensure family engagement opportunities are meaningful.

- **Link to learning:** Go beyond sharing what students are learning in the classroom, to sharing strategies families can use at home that are directly linked to the skills students need to learn at their age and grade level.
- **Build relationships:** Develop trust and respect, which includes listening to parents and caregivers' concerns and ideas, as well as understanding home cultures and the interests students bring with them to the classroom.
- **Develop dual capacity:** Provide training and professional development for teachers and families together.

Take inventory of all the ways you engage families. Then consider the following questions to assess if your family engagement approach incorporates Henderson and Mapp's (2002) strategies.

1. Are they accessible to all the families in my classroom? What time and days do they happen? Are there multiple times and ways for parents and caregivers to volunteer, for example?
2. Who tends to attend and participate, and who doesn't? What kinds of outreach have I done to ensure greater participation? Have I asked parents and caregivers what would work for them?
3. Have I asked what families need, or what their concerns are? Are my family engagement opportunities meeting these needs and concerns?
4. Do these opportunities address student learning and student achievement goals? Am I sharing strategies with families? Am I learning strategies from families?
5. Do the schoolwide family engagement events provide any opportunities for parents and teachers to collaborate or learn together?

A Learning Experience

Through the surveys and interviews I conducted with parents (majority White) of first and second graders at my school (see chapter 3, page 43), I learned that most parents were silent about race and racism because they didn't know how to talk to their kids about the subject—they were learning, too.

I was interested to find out what would make White parents feel more competent in talking about race and racism. Two key factors stood out as contributing to a sense of competency:

1. Applying a growth mindset to the discussions (Dweck, 2017). Making mistakes is part of growth and does not mean you're a "bad" person.
2. Accessing school-led trainings and communications from teachers about social and academic experiences in the classroom. Parents were willing to use the words, if these words were supplied by those they viewed as experts, such as teachers and administrators.

Prior to this research project, I had focused on providing the foundational knowledge my students needed to have effective and inclusive classroom conversations about racism and to change the dynamic in my classroom. Once I learned more about the nature of silence among White families, and my potential as an educator to grow their competency levels, I began to understand more fully the value of including families in this learning. Through that experience, I committed to moving from a reactive to a proactive stance with parents and caregivers.

A Change From Reactive to Proactive

Teachers make it a practice to reach out to family members when a student is struggling academically. If a student can't identify all the letters in the alphabet, or recognize numbers, or regulate their emotions, or manage conflicts with their peers, teachers and parents collaborate to help the child make progress. These are the areas of teaching and learning that most parents and caregivers can easily get behind: the building blocks of academic education and the social and emotional well-being of their child.

Not all parents and early childhood educators place the same value on teaching about race and racism. Often, teachers need to make the case for this type of learning, either because parents or colleagues think students are too young or that the subject matter belongs at home. How can teachers take a proactive stance toward building respect and trust with families around this topic? Before discussing specific practices, I'd like to share some resources you can look to for support.

- **The National Association for the Education of Young Children (NAEYC):** NAEYC offers information for early childhood educators about antibias education in the form of articles, magazines, and books. Use these resources to communicate to parents how antibias curricula support identity development and foster equity in the classroom.
- **EmbraceRace:** EmbraceRace was founded in early 2016 by two parents hoping to create a community around raising kids in a world

where race matters. Educators can use these resources, specifically catered to parents and caregivers, to engage with families around race. Their Race and Early Childhood section offers tips, articles, books, and webinars on many topics related to race and learning. For example, how to support Black and Indigenous children of color, and how to identify biases in children and what to do about them.

- **Action guides:** EmbraceRace's action guides are designed to "help parents of all backgrounds teach and talk to their children about race early and often by highlighting age-appropriate activities that can easily be incorporated into daily life" (EmbraceRace, & MomsRising, n.d.). Their "10 Tips for Teaching and Talking to Kids About Race" (EmbraceRace, & MomsRising, n.d.) is a set of clear, concrete steps educators and parents can take right away, based on the research behind what young students need to develop strong, antiracist identities. This is a great handout to provide at beginning-of-the-year events, such as parent conferences or back-to-school nights.

At your first parent-teacher conference, try distributing a pamphlet or article about antibias education, published by NAEYC or EmbraceRace, and discuss these ideas and how you apply them with students. This could sound like, "Current research shows that young children notice the differences around them and pick up on societal biases about these differences. The way I respond to that research is to talk openly in class about these differences, as well as many similarities, so that we can learn what they mean and how to be respectful with one another."

Parents and caregivers should know the science, or data, behind the antibias approach, and they should know your goals in adopting this teaching. Always invite parents and caregivers to share questions or input. This is a great way to talk through some of their concerns or to hear their suggestions. Taking this proactive stance may help you avoid having to manage anxiety or defensiveness about a problem with a student down the road.

Incorporate this focus on teaching about differences and similarities, and the work on changemakers and social justice, into each family engagement opportunity. This could include events like back-to-school nights or open houses, notes home, and monthly newsletters that spotlight various aspects of the curriculum. Try as much as possible to include student voices in these sharings so that parents and caregivers can see and hear what the learning looks and sounds like in the classroom.

In addition to these general resources and guidelines, I'd like to share some specific initiatives you can incorporate into your family engagement practices.

Create Family Book Bags

One way to encourage families to have proactive discussions about race at home is to create book bags that families can check out from the library. Based on your school's resources, these bags may include various picture books, suggested questions for discussion, and glossary terms when necessary. Figure 8.1 is an example of a letter we send home in these book bags.

Dear Families,

The intent of this specific family book bag is to provide elementary literature that will invite conversation, stimulate curiosity, and result in deep dialogue at home around race and social justice. Over time, we'd like to develop new family book bags around other topics that support our self-awareness and knowledge building about cultural identities represented in our school community and around the world.

We are committed to developing empathy through literature. Included in this family book is a beloved book, *All the Colors We Are*, along with questions to guide your family as you read and discuss. In addition, there is an *optional* page for students to draw a picture or share their thoughts in writing about the books they read and the conversation they had at home regarding race and social justice. *Please feel free to share other book titles that you have found to be engaging for elementary school children regarding race and social justice. We can be resources for one another.*

All the Colors We Are, written in both English and Spanish, is a scientific explanation that illustrates the role melanin plays in the color of our skin. As people migrated farther from the equator millions of years ago, the people with lighter skin/less melanin were more able to survive farther from the equator. This adaptation led to the variety of skin colors represented from the equator poles. It wasn't until recent history that people used these skin color differences to justify unequal treatment. The book provides an opportunity to discuss that not all parents and children are biologically related. Reflecting on this one aspect of where the color of our skin comes from can include ancestors we may not know or know about. Biological ancestors might be different between children, parents, and siblings. There are lots of ways to make a family.

What color is your skin? What would you like to name the color of your skin? Can you come up with a name for each shade of skin color in your family?

Do you think that your family's ancestors from a long time ago came from a warm, sunny place or from a cooler place with less sunshine? Did some come from a warm place and others from a cooler place? Why do you think this?

How does this story change what you know about skin color?

Figure 8.1: Sample letter to include in family book bags.

Involve Families in the Peaceful Changemakers Discussion

When my students and I discuss peaceful changemakers in kindergarten, we, as a class, look for them everywhere. We find them in books, in one another, and through our study of famous people such as Dr. Maathai and Dr. King. To make this learning personal and meaningful for students, the kindergarten teaching team also asks students to talk to their parents and caregivers about people in their families or communities who work to make the world a better place. Over the years, students have chosen to honor a range of changemakers—from siblings, to grandparents, to neighbors, to distant relatives or ancestors.

Whenever possible, we ask that students and families bring their changemakers into the class so that we can all learn about the diverse ways people are working to make positive change, and all the different ages, races, and genders represented. Students practice asking questions and giving positive, affirming feedback to our visitors, which often sounds like, "Thank you for sharing. We learned a lot!" This is also a great time to practice making connections between changemakers and using the windows and mirrors frame to notice similarities and differences. Figure 8.2 is an example of a letter we send home around this project.

Dear Families,

In kindergarten, we are celebrating peaceful changemakers, or people who use nonviolent strategies to bring about positive change for their communities and around the world. We are asking each family to honor someone in their family or in their community who works for positive change. Please take some time to talk with your child about this person. Each child should bring a **short**, written statement about their person (a statement written by a parent is fine) and a photo, printed image, or drawing of their person. In our classroom we will have a large chart that will visually organize the life and work of the people we are studying as a class. We encourage you to use the chart to guide your discussions

continued →

with your child. We are excited to learn all about the people around us who work to make the world a better place!

We would also like to open our classrooms to any families that are interested in presenting their person of change to our class, or bringing their person if this is possible. **This is entirely optional**. Please let us know if you would be interested in presenting.

Thank you!

Kindergarten Teachers

Figure 8.2: Sample letter to invite families to share about a peaceful changemaker.

The Value of Conversations With Families

I've already shared how implementing the changemaker curriculum and antiracist teaching in my classroom addressed the challenge of White students dominating conversations about Dr. King (chapter 7, page 109).

When I asked Black families in my class for their input, it initiated additional shifts to that dynamic. I asked families what the experience of talking about Dr. King's birthday had been like for their child in preschool, what they wanted the experience to be like in kindergarten, what their child already knew about the topic, and what they wanted them to know. Families reported that they wanted their children to feel confident and empowered, and they didn't want the conversation to make their child feel victimized or singled out, the way some of them had felt in preschool around Dr. King's birthday.

One family sent in a bag of books, which is how I discovered Johnny Ray Moore's (2015) *The Story of Martin Luther King Jr.* You read in chapter 7 (page 109) about how Jessica, whose family sent in the bag of books, was the first to speak up during our discussion about Dr. King. I now read the book with students every year. She introduced the book to the class and talked about what she loved about it. Including her family in my teaching had empowered her to participate and share her knowledge.

I didn't always value this kind of two-way communication and learning from families. I used to feel my role was to provide information and to answer questions. The experience of reaching out to Black families showed me that inviting families to shape the learning environment is extremely valuable. Today, my family engagement strategies involve reaching out to all families multiple times throughout the year. This includes asking what their child knows about Dr. King, whether they'd like to come into the classroom to share about their family, and if they'd like to teach the class about someone in their family or community who is a peaceful changemaker. This kind of collaboration allows students to feel they are seen and valued at school. As Derman-Sparks and Edwards (2020) write in *Anti-Bias Education for Young Children and Ourselves,* "Feeling a sense of belonging will support children in coming to trust the environment, form strong attachments, and explore and learn" (p. 379). A respectful, mutual collaboration between teachers and families about race and racism can lead to a more unified, antiracist classroom community in which every member and their families are committed to combating bias and racism.

To create bonds with families that are inclusive and truly collaborative, teachers must critically examine their family engagement initiatives to ensure they are not perpetuating exclusionary practices. Unexamined practices rooted in systems designed to serve White students and White families at the exclusion of others will continue if we don't replace them with equitable and inclusive practices. This critical examination, or as Adams (2014) called it, *soul searching*, can result in real change so that every family feels like they belong, in your classroom and in your wider school community.

CHAPTER 9

COMMON ROADBLOCKS AND A PATH THROUGH THEM

In chapter 1 (page 13), you read about Nottingham's (2017) strategy, called *the pit*, for encouraging students to welcome and explore contradictions and uncertainties as part of the learning process. I'd like to revisit that here and think about how it applies for teachers and students embracing antiracist practices in the classroom.

The pit is about cognitive dissonance, about having multiple, conflicting ideas at the same time. Nottingham (2017) writes:

> The pit represents moving beyond a single, basic idea into the situation of having multiple ideas that are as yet unsorted. This happens when a learner purposefully explores inconsistencies, exceptions and contradictions in their own or others' thinking so as to discover a richer, more complex understanding. (p. 7)

It is not a comfortable place to be. In fact, most of us want to get out of the pit as soon as we land in it: things don't seem to make sense, it's hard to find clarity, and we don't feel a mastery of the concepts and ideas.

But it is precisely these moments of discomfort that offer students of any age the most powerful learning. Nottingham (2017) compares the discomfort associated with being in the pit to the experience of learning how to ride a bike: you may practice with your training wheels on at first to feel stable and successful. When the training wheels come off, you wobble, which can be unsettling and scary. Or think about a toddler learning to walk. First, they hold on to the edge of a table or the back of a chair, then they take a step or two, then they walk across the room.

Each new experience is a challenge, is inherently uncomfortable—and yet, this is essential for growth and development.

If getting into the pit is about creating cognitive conflicts, then teaching about race and racism gets us into the pit right away. Cognitive conflict occurs nearly every time we talk about race. Unlike skin color, race is a social construct, and yet it has real meaning in our culture in terms of how racial categories have been used to oppress people of color. The discomfort that can arise in these conversations often feels especially difficult.

I've had numerous conversations with my daughters where I've felt physically uncomfortable—my heart races and my temples buzz. But turning away from my daughters in these moments, retreating into comfort by denying what they were discovering, thinking about, questioning, and trying to understand, would have meant leaving them. I couldn't jump out of the pit while they were still there figuring it out.

In those moments of discomfort, I've learned to take deep breaths, locate where in my body I feel discomfort, and breathe into those places. I engage in positive self-talk, "You can do this," and I focus on my goals. In difficult conversations with my daughters, my goal is always to support their growing understandings, to be their ally, and to listen. When I choose this response to discomfort, I'm able to hear their concerns and questions more clearly, to take a moment to think about how I want to respond, and to stay present and engaged. When you are in the midst of a difficult conversation with a student, or with your class, what might it look like for you to lean on these tools, center your goals, and move through any discomfort you may feel?

As a White person, I have the privilege to ignore race, to make it about something else, to pretend as if we live in a color-blind or post-racial society. My daughters don't have this privilege. As their mom, I actively choose to stay present in uncomfortable situations, to let conversations happen, to listen to their questions, to affirm what they are experiencing, and to be honest about answers I don't have.

As I conducted interviews with White parents in the course of my research, I found that those who initiated conversations about race and racism also tended to be in a close relationship with a person of color: a child, partner, or family member. When I asked what kept them engaged even when it was hard, they said things like, "It's not about my own comfort, it's about supporting the people I love." This may be helpful for teachers confronting their discomfort with conversations about race and racism. Sticking with hard conversations even when you feel uncomfortable is a way to support your students, whose growing understanding of race and racism will allow them to be antiracist. It will also support your own personal commitment to justice and equity, which necessarily requires moments of discomfort.

As you teach about race and racism, you will invariably run into roadblocks, some more challenging than others. The tools we can access for working through these challenges are similar to those we use to face challenges in academic instruction, emotional regulation, and conflict resolution. Teaching is a process of trying things, reflecting, making adjustments, trying again, reflecting, and on and on. When we find a strategy or approach or piece of curriculum that seems to work every time, we feel a sense of relief until we have a student or a class for whom it doesn't work at all. Then, we try something else. This is true for every area of teaching. It's part of what keeps the work alive and engaging. We are always working in direct relationship with our students, and doing our best means responding to their needs.

It's important to remember that you will have experiences that make you question the validity of teaching about race and racism. Not many parents or school leaders question the validity of teaching children how to read or how to develop number sense. More schools are also adopting formal social-emotional learning curricula. And yet, not many of these social-emotional learning programs incorporate explicit teaching about race and racism. Many are a one-size-fits-all model or may even employ a color-blind approach (Caven, 2020).

You may find it's necessary to make the case to your colleagues, or to parents and caregivers, for teaching about race, as well as about skin color, gender, and other differences. Not everyone in your school community may be on board with this. Building competency may be the place to start, whether that's through sharing book titles and articles (see appendix C, page 161, for a list of resources). Or you may begin by sharing the research you've encountered in this book, demonstrating that young students notice race, that anti-Black bias remains prevalent in society, that antibias teaching can decrease bias and increase empathy and cooperation. Regardless of where you start or how you proceed, you can be sure that you'll face roadblocks along the way.

In this chapter, we'll look at five common roadblocks: (1) challenges from colleagues, (2) concern from parents or caregivers, (3) uncomfortable questions or statements from students, (4) bias in the classroom, and (5) personal mistakes. I'll share personal stories and strategies for overcoming these challenges.

Ultimately, teachers can't account for every circumstance they'll face in antiracist teaching; sometimes the best thing they can do is ask for help.

Roadblock 1: Challenges From Colleagues

One year, as I taught a lesson on racial justice changemakers, a visiting teacher observed the lesson. That day we learned about Ruby Bridges and Claudette Colvin, two young people who challenged segregation and racist practices in brave and important ways. As we previously discussed, Bridges was the first elementary school student to integrate a school in the South at six years old, and Colvin refused to give up her bus seat for a White person. After the lesson, the visiting teacher pulled me aside and said, "Isn't this all just too conceptual for your students? Do you think they really get all of this?"

I felt myself getting defensive. I thought about showing her some of the work they'd been doing, their writing about being a changemaker, the issues they cared deeply about and wanted to improve, but I didn't. I wasn't sure it would help her understand what I felt to be true: that by learning about people of all races, ages, and genders who work to solve social problems, my students were learning how to see possible paths forward for themselves. Instead, I responded with a metaphor about planting seeds. I acknowledged that some of the concepts may be difficult for young students to *fully* grasp, but that didn't mean I shouldn't introduce them. I didn't convince her of my approach, but that ultimately wasn't the point. The point was to share my perspective of what I was hoping to gain by teaching about changemakers.

That conversation stays with me because it was also a good reminder to make sure that my students were *doing* as much as they were talking about making positive changes. The visiting teacher had a point: students don't always do their best learning when the learning is too conceptual, too much about sitting and listening and having discussions. Young students need the opportunity to try things out, to actively engage with their learning. I made sure there were multiple opportunities for active learning, whether this was in the form of field trips to work with local environmental organizations or cross-grade-level buddy experiences to make art that incorporated messages of activism.

If you experience a similar roadblock or challenge to your teaching, touch in with your goals and filter the challenge through the lens of those goals. Consider keeping a reflection journal in which you record lesson objectives and outcomes, as well as collect data of some kind throughout your instruction. Pre- and post-learning assessments can help signify what gains your students have made and where there's still room for growth and understanding. This has the dual benefit of informing your own instruction and communicating the benefits of the instruction to those who challenge it.

Roadblock 2: Concern From Parents or Caregivers

The day after I read *The Story of Ruby Bridges* by Robert Coles (2010) to my class, a student's mother came into my classroom visibly upset. She was a White mother of a biracial child, and her daughter, Samantha, had come home talking about the book—but the parent hadn't wanted her child to learn about racism yet. She said she had purposefully not told her daughter anything about race, with the hope that her sense of identity would not be compromised, that she wouldn't feel different from anyone else, and that she wouldn't see the world in terms of categories but in terms of sameness and a shared humanity. This mother was expressing her desire to raise a color-blind child, and I had just disrupted her dream. Her daughter had used words like "White" and "Black" for the first time. She worried that the conversations in my classroom were going to make her daughter feel bad, victimized, or less than in some way. She was expressing fears similar to the ones I had had for years—the reasons for my own silence around this topic.

I felt some doubt creep in. *Was* it a good idea to tell these kinds of ugly truths to young children? Were my students actually too young for these conversations? Was I spoiling their innocence, or their ability to see the good and potential in everyone?

I thought back to Samantha's behavior and comments the day before as I read the book. Samantha sat at the back of the carpet carefully listening as I read. When I got to the page that showed Ruby Bridges sitting alone at her desk, Samantha stood up, one hand in the air. "This is unfair!" she said. "This is wrong! We have to do something about this." Before sitting back down, she continued, "They are just staying home from school because she has brown skin. This is not right." Other students nodded in agreement, and I said, "You're right. This is called racism, and it is wrong and unfair. And, I agree, we need to always fight against it." Samantha nodded fervently. "I will," she said, sitting down. Others called out, "Me, too." Another child offered, "This is why she's a changemaker." And another said, "We need to have courage like Ruby Bridges so we can be changemakers."

I shared all of this with Samantha's mother. I reassured her that Samantha had left the classroom empowered to work toward making the world a better place, rather than feeling sad or victimized. She relaxed as I talked. At the end of our conversation, she asked if she could borrow the book so they could read it together as a family.

Sometimes the most powerful way to work through a roadblock with a parent or caregiver is simply to share a story about a student. One way to prepare for this is to keep notes on what your students say during conversations about race and racism. These notes can help you gain a deeper appreciation for what they are understanding or reteach a concept they struggled with. Also, there is something powerful about sharing the actual words students use, especially when a parent is unsure if the topic is appropriate for their child. Knowing that their child is saying things like, "We need to change this!" and "Everyone should be included!" can help ease their fears and allow them to trust the process.

Roadblock 3: Uncomfortable Questions or Statements From Students

When given the opportunity, young students will ask many, many questions about the world and how it works. You may be able to answer some of these questions, depending on your expertise and knowledge base. I know there have been plenty of times I've had to say to a student, "I don't know the answer to that."

When it comes to answering questions that come up during conversations about race and racism, teachers don't always give themselves permission to say, "I don't know" because they feel they need to have the answers right then and there. Regardless of how well you break down complicated concepts, students will inevitably ask challenging, deep questions about race and racism that you can't answer, at least not right away. Sometimes, the best thing to do is simply to say, "I don't know the answer to that question, and I'm so glad you asked it. Let me do some more thinking and research and get back to you." It's important to return to the student before too much time has passed, in order to let the student know that you mean what you say, take their questions seriously, and want to answer them as truthfully as possible.

Sometimes the challenge isn't a question you're unsure how to answer, but a statement that you're not sure how to respond to. One afternoon, in the middle of listening to the story *The Power of Her Pen: The Story of Groundbreaking Journalist Ethel L. Payne* by Lesa Cline-Ransome (2020), one student, James, said, "I feel left out. We keep talking about Black people and women." I was caught off guard, I hadn't been expecting this, and it made me wonder if other students were having similar feelings.

I said, "Thank you for being brave and sharing how you're feeling. That's so important for us to know. In this class, we want all of you to feel equally cared about because we care about you all the same, no matter what you look like, your race, or your gender. It is also our job, the teachers at this school, to tell you stories that haven't been told before. That's why we tell stories of Black people and talk about women's rights. For many, many years, these stories weren't told in schools. Remember Marley Dias? She wanted to get books, at her school and schools around the country, that featured Black girls as main characters. That's the work we are doing in our classroom, too."

One way to ensure that each student in your class is feeling included, valued, and seen is to invite their families into your class, a family engagement strategy I explored in the previous chapter. You can invite families to share about special traditions, or what they like to do together, or who makes up their family. Families can bring in photos in the form of a slide show, a poster, or in a photo album; they can also bring in other meaningful artifacts. The key to this family project is to make sure it is accessible to all families, which requires being flexible about how and when families are invited to share.

James's family visited our class, he introduced them to us, and he talked about their favorite things to do together and where in the country their extended family lived. After James was able to share his family with the class, he no longer talked about feeling left out.

Roadblock 4: Bias in the Classroom

When a student says or does something biased, it's tempting to shush them without explaining what's wrong with what he or she said or did. The student may learn not to say or act that way when the teacher is present, but that doesn't mean they won't do it when they're out of earshot. In that situation, the student needs the right information to understand why their action or words were biased and incorrect. If a student continues to be biased in their comments or actions after these kinds of explanations, a teacher may need to intervene further by meeting with the students' other teachers and family to create a strategy for addressing the behavior.

Another way to handle bias in the moment it occurs is to remind your students of class agreements you've come up with together in the form of a class charter or a set of community guidelines. You can activate their empathy by asking them how they would feel if these words were said to them. It's also important to pay attention to the impact rather than the intent of the person who said the biased comment. You can do this by focusing on the student who received the bias, checking in with them, making sure they are OK, and helping the other student to recognize the impact of their words. Have the student help you solve the problem by figuring out what the other student needs. This could be an apology or a commitment to not do it again.

A fourth-grade teacher recently shared with me how she handles moments of bias in her majority White classroom. She said she's always thinking about the best ways to support her Black students, especially in conversations about race and racism. "I don't want to shame students," she told me. "But sometimes White students will say things that I need to call out in the moment. I'll say things like, 'You are minimizing a situation that should not be minimized.'" Sometimes, though, a comment is so shocking she doesn't know how to respond right away. One time, after she read a story about Harriet Tubman, one of her students said, "If I were a slave owner, I'd treat people better. I'd be a better slave owner." She told me, "I didn't know what to say. I needed time to process. I wasn't sure if I should say something just to that student or to the whole class. I decided I needed to come back to the whole class. Supporting my Black students was about being honest and addressing it with everyone." She said it was important for her to also acknowledge her own silence. She started with, "I feel responsible for not addressing this fully at the time it happened, but I'd like to do it now. Bodies are not to be owned."

Roadblock 5: Personal Mistakes

There have been plenty of times I wished I could grab my words out of the air and swallow them. I knew as soon as the words came out that they were not the right words, the ones that would lead to a greater understanding or connection.

When a student once told me that he noticed Black people when he saw homeless people, I wanted to correct his thinking right away. I was aware of all the problems with how he was understanding race: He thought Black people were necessarily homeless. He wasn't noticing the Black students in the classroom. He wasn't thinking about how this comment would affect them. Because I couldn't think of a simple sentence that would communicate all of that, I didn't say anything at all, at first. I took some time, and some breaths, and said, "You and I need to talk more about this so we can understand what you're seeing and noticing. It's also true that there are many, many Black people who are not homeless but who may not live in your neighborhood, and it's possible you haven't traveled to their neighborhoods." This response let the student know that something important and problematic was happening in the way he was seeing race, and that I cared enough about it that I wanted to revisit the conversation and work together to grow his understanding.

That student's comment fit a pattern I'd noticed of White students connecting Blackness solely with poverty, and specifically, homelessness, without also recognizing systemic racism, a pattern that disturbed me as an educator and parent of Black girls. It took some time for me to come back to him and have a more nuanced conversation about systemic racism, generational wealth, and the media's portrayal of Black people. I didn't discuss it with the whole class, though in hindsight I regret that. As the fourth-grade teacher said, supporting the students of color in my classroom would have meant being honest and transparent with everyone, to say, "I take responsibility for not addressing this sooner, and I want to do it now."

When teachers aren't sure what to say or they retreat into silence in response to a tough moment, it's helpful to have a pool of resources to draw from to determine next steps. This is especially helpful when the resources are fun, encouraging, and promote a growth mindset. I've had a lot of success with songs and videos. In chapter 1 (page 13), you read about *Sesame Street's* (2014b) "Power of Yet." The music video features a cast of *Sesame Street* characters who are struggling to master new skills and want to give up until Janelle Monáe tells them about a special power: the power of "yet." This is a great resource you can share with students in moments when they may be struggling with their learning around race and racism. Consider the following list of other great *Sesame Street* resources to add to your tool kit.

- "I Love My Hair" (*Sesame Street*, 2010)
- "Lupita Nyong'o Loves Her Skin" (*Sesame Street*, 2014c)
- "Skin Song" (*Sesame Street*, n.d.)
- "The Color of Me" (PA Upload, 2021)
- "Mark Ruffalo: Empathy" (*Sesame Street*, 2011)

In addition to songs and videos, books (of course) are a teacher's best friend. When you are not sure how to address a question from a student or how to break down a complex topic into terms your young students will understand, sometimes the best thing to do is read a picture book without much explanation. Appendix B (page 157) contains a list of picture books that address skin color, race, hair, and other identity pieces. In addition to those, I can recommend the Netflix special, *Bookmarks*, developed by Marley Dias (Collins et al., 2020). It's a wonderful resource for finding great books that celebrate Blackness. Each book is read aloud by the author or a Black celebrity, and each video ends with a question for the students to consider, which can lead seamlessly into writing and drawing activities as well.

Roadblocks are difficult and can make us want to retreat to areas of instruction that feel less complicated or that we have greater mastery over. Yet, if we are to join the movement toward greater equity within our educational institutions, and if we are dedicated to giving students the skills they need to become antiracist changemakers themselves, we must find ways to confront these challenges and stay in conversation rather than retreat to silence.

Table 9.1 shows a summary of the roadblocks, strategies, and examples we've discussed in this chapter.

TABLE 9.1: At-a-Glance Reference for Roadblocks, Sample Strategies, and Examples

Roadblock	Strategy to Try	Example
Challenges From Colleagues	Acknowledge that some of the concepts may be difficult for young students to *fully* grasp, but that doesn't mean they shouldn't be introduced to them. Provide opportunities for students to try things out and to actively engage with their learning (versus sitting, listening, and having discussions).	When teaching about changemakers, take students on field trips to work with local environmental organizations. Try organizing cross-grade-level buddy experiences to make art that incorporates messages of activism.
Challenges From Parents or Caregivers	Share a story about a student during conversations about race and racism.	Share with a concerned parent or caregiver specific words that students said during these conversations (for example, "We need to change this!" or "Everyone should be included!"). This can help ease their fears and allow them to trust the process.

Uncomfortable Questions or Statements From Students	*For a challenging question:* Give yourself permission to say, "I don't know." Return to the student before too much time has passed to let the student know you mean what you say, you take their questions seriously, and you want to answer them as honestly and truthfully as possible. *For a challenging statement:* Communicate that you appreciate their honesty and that they can always communicate how they feel. *For challenging questions or statements:* Invite students' families into your class to share about special traditions, what they like to do together, or who makes up their family. Make sure this activity is accessible to all families. Be flexible about how and when families are invited to share.	*For a challenging question:* "I don't know the answer to that question, and I'm so glad you asked it. Let me do some more thinking and research and get back to you." *For a challenging statement:* "People of all races work to solve racism. It's our job to learn from this and not repeat it, especially those of us who are White, to work against racism." "Thank you for being brave and sharing how you're feeling. In this class we want all of you to feel equally cared about because we care about you all the same, no matter what you look like, your race, or your gender. It is also our job, the teachers at this school, to tell you stories that haven't been told before. That's why we tell Black people's stories and talk about women's rights. For many, many years, these stories weren't told in schools."
Bias in the Classroom	Replace their biased action with something else (in many cases, the right information, in order to decrease the bias). Remind your students of class agreements you've come up with together in the form of a class charter or a set of community guidelines. Pay attention to the *impact* rather than the *intent* of the person who said the biased comment. You can do this by focusing on the student who received the bias, checking in with them, making sure they are OK, and having the other student recognize the impact of their words. Have the student help you solve the problem by figuring out what the other student needs, which could be an apology or a commitment to not doing it again	"It's not OK to touch anyone's hair because the oil on our fingers can dry the hair out, because sometimes people take a lot of time with their hair and it's not OK to mess that up, and it's never OK to touch a friend without permission." "You are minimizing a situation that should not be minimized."
Personal Mistakes	Give yourself permission to address the topic again with the student and class.	"I take responsibility for not addressing this sooner, and I want to do it now."

The Path Beyond the Roadblocks

Encountering roadblocks along the way to incorporating antiracist practices into the classroom is inevitable. The five we've discussed in this chapter are common to many teachers engaging in this work, but you'll likely face many more that we haven't named here. When in doubt, ask for help.

When I first asked families in my classroom what their children already knew about Dr. King and what they wanted them to learn, I realize I was asking for help. I didn't see it that way at the time, but their feedback and contributions were invaluable in helping me improve my instruction. The Peaceful Changemaker Curriculum came about because I asked my colleagues what their experiences were like around teaching about Dr. King, and it turned out they needed as much help as I did to improve the experience for their students. This path is much easier to walk when you're not doing it alone.

You will face tough challenges, self-doubt, and uncertainty along the way. But through it all, remember why you are doing this work. You are supporting young students to change the narrative around race, celebrate similarities and differences, communicate with respect across these differences, and recognize and combat biases when they arise. You are creating a classroom where every student is equipped with the truth about race and the tools to work toward greater justice and equity.

GLOSSARY

Color blindness — The desire to see beyond race, to see others as individuals, "human to human" (DiAngelo, 2012)

Cultural competence — A set of congruent behaviors, attitudes, and policies that come together in a system, agency, or among professionals and enable that system, agency, or those professionals to work effectively in cross-cultural situations (Lee, 2018)

Implicit bias — Unconscious negative associations people hold and automatically express (Staats, 2013)

Inclusion — Bringing traditionally marginalized people or groups into communities, positions, processes, and structures in a way that offers belonging and shares power (Racial Equity Tools, 2020)

Microaggressions — The everyday verbal, nonverbal, and environmental slights, snubs, or insults, whether intentional or unintentional, that communicate hostile, derogatory, or negative messages to target persons based solely upon their marginalized group membership (Sue et al., 2007)

Race — A social construct as opposed to biological fact, dynamic and ongoing, relational and systemic; there is no "race neutral" space (Kivel, 2017); a power construct of collected or merged difference that lives socially (Kendi, 2019)

Racial literacy	The ability to read, recast, and resolve racially stressful social interactions (H. Stevenson, 2014)
Racism	Marriage of racist policies and racist ideas that produces and normalizes racial inequities (Kendi, 2019); different from prejudice or discrimination because it is based upon one group having the power to carry out systematic discrimination
White supremacy culture	Dominant, unquestioned standards of behavior and ways of functioning accepted by the majority of U.S. institutions, evolved from U.S. history of White supremacy (Gulati-Partee & Potapchuk, 2014)

APPENDIX A

FREQUENTLY ASKED QUESTIONS

Teachers implementing antiracist practices in the classroom frequently receive questions from parents and colleagues. This appendix contains common questions and answers teachers may receive as they begin talking to students about race and racism.

Questions From Parents and Caregivers

1. *Why are you talking about race in kindergarten?*

Young children notice differences and try to make sense of them before they enter kindergarten. Research shows that babies as young as six months old notice skin color differences and can begin to display same-race preferences as early as nine months (Xiao et al., 2017). In order to help young children understand what differences mean (including skin color differences and race differences) and to prevent biases and prejudices from forming, they need the opportunity to talk about these differences, learn the facts, and learn how to communicate respectfully with one another across differences.

Talking about race in kindergarten is a multilayered approach that includes learning where skin color comes from and how it is different from race, checking our biases and assumptions about skin color, engaging in antibias activities such as art projects and picture books that celebrate the color brown, and critically examining our classroom materials and curriculum to ensure that Whiteness is not centralized. This is part of building a strong, unified, antiracist classroom community. We need to talk about race to help our young students learn how to be antiracists.

2. *Do you really think a five-year-old is capable of understanding things as complex as empathy, discrimination, or justice?*

At five years old, students are beginning to develop a strong sense of fairness and equity (Derman-Sparks & Edwards, 2020). They are becoming aware of their larger community and world, and their place within it. At this age, students are often quick to point out when something isn't fair for them or others. Additionally, they are often quick to aid and comfort a hurt or upset peer. They are also often eager to talk about what it means to be kind, inclusive, and empathetic. Because young children learn best by doing and through explicit practice, it's most effective when these ideas are put into practice right away. Teachers can use puppet plays, acting out scenarios, examining characters in books, and other strategies for how to be empathetic and inclusive.

When problems occur on the playground or in the classroom, we bring these social-emotional tools to the problem solving. This could sound like, "How would we use our empathy tool to help Sam right now? If we think about how Sam is feeling, that can help us figure out what he needs." This is important because five- and six-year-olds are often quite good at giving the "right" answer during class discussions about social-emotional skills, but in a moment of conflict, they can revert to self-centered behavior. The more practice they have learning about emotions, recognizing emotions in others, and using the social and emotional tools or skills they learn about in lessons, the better equipped they will be to solve problems peacefully.

3. *Isn't my child too young for this kind of instruction?*

Young children notice differences, including race and inequities across racial lines, regardless of whether we explicitly talk about these issues in the classroom (Aboud, 2008). This is true for children in racially heterogeneous and racially homogenous schools. The danger in waiting to talk about race and racism until a child reaches an age deemed more appropriate for this learning is that this child has most likely already formed some biased and misinformed ideas about race (Xiao et al., 2017). The way that we talk about these issues in kindergarten should be based on knowledge about what young children need to know about race and other identities in order to be prepared to have more complex and nuanced understandings in upper grades. The teacher's job is to lay a foundation of understanding, similar to the way we ensure that students have solid number sense or a strong grasp of the alphabet before we move on to algebra or reading chapter books.

The young student who leaves kindergarten knowing what skin color is and what it isn't, aware of the dangers of making assumptions about people based on differences and how racial categories were invented to oppress people of color, is much better prepared to be antiracist than the young child who is never allowed to ask their questions, check their own biases, and learn the truth about race and racism.

4. *Shouldn't this type of discussion happen at home?*

Yes, discussions about race and racism *should* happen at home and often do. But research shows that many White parents don't initiate such conversations, and especially not with young children (Bronson & Merryman, 2009; Vittrup, 2016). When some students come to school well versed in issues of race and racism and others don't, issues can arise on the playground and in the classroom that lead to exclusionary and biased behavior.

Part of fostering antiracism in all students is decentralizing Whiteness, which necessarily involves talking about what Whiteness is and where it comes from as a racial category invented to oppress people of color. It's important to emphasize that the story of race and racism belongs to, and is about, all of us. It is our responsibility, especially those of us who identify as White, to work to solve this problem, which necessarily involves talking about it at home and at school.

5. *Will talking about race create divisions between students?*

The fear that talking about differences will cause divisions between students is based on the idea that the most inclusive child is the color blind child—the child who doesn't see race. Research tells us that all children notice differences, whether they voice these observations out loud, and exhibit same-race preferences at a young age (Winkler, 2009; Xiao et al., 2017). Still, to promote color blindness, or to dissuade young children from this kind of noticing, parents and teachers tend to shush a young child when noticing an observed difference, trying to promote inclusion by emphasizing all the ways we are the same and ignoring our differences. While often well intentioned, the problem with this approach is that shushing young children does not stop them from noticing, it just leaves them alone to make sense of these differences, and their conclusions are often misinformed or biased.

A truly inclusive approach is one in which parents and teachers don't shy away from talking openly about differences, including race. We must proactively engage with young children about these issues in a way that gives factual information and emphasizes the danger of making assumptions based on differences.

Using the windows and mirrors frame, developed by Bishop (1990), is a helpful way to emphasize all the ways we are the same and different. You can talk about differences with others as the experience of looking out of a window and being curious about seeing something new, and similarities as looking into a mirror and seeing yourself reflected. This helps young children understand that we can have windows and mirrors with everyone, including people in our own families, and people who we may think are very different from us. Emphasizing all the ways that we are the same and different is one way to ensure that children don't divide themselves based on perceived shared attributes. In addition, teachers and parents can talk explicitly about the dangers of excluding others based on differences, and give students opportunities to role-play with puppets or act out scenarios of exclusion and problem solve together.

6. *Why are you teaching about Black Lives Matter in the classroom? Shouldn't children be taught that all lives matter?*

This question is based on the false idea that teaching about Black Lives Matter is implicitly teaching that all lives *don't* matter. Through the Black Lives Matter movement, young students learn about skin color differences and how racial categories were invented to oppress people of color as a continuation of the struggle for civil and human rights.

When teachers talk about Black Lives Matter in the classroom, they should emphasize that teachers care about all students, that all their lives matter to us a great deal. We can tell our students that as long as there is racism and bias, we have to say Black Lives Matter in order to continue to work toward equity and justice. For too long, in many schools, especially across the United States, teaching about race and racism has emphasized the gains of the civil rights movement without also telling the truth about how racism continues to operate in visible and invisible ways. We see this in police killings of Black and Brown people, racist rhetoric reentering our discourse, the reversal of key voter protection acts in many states, and other similar events. To foster antiracism in all students, we have to let them know how the problem continues, and how we can all work together to solve it.

Questions From Colleagues

1. *Where do I find the time for this type of instruction?*

For many years, educational leaders did not consider social-emotional learning (SEL) a valuable, core part of instruction. At the time of this writing, twenty states have adopted SEL competencies for their K–12 programs (Collaborative for Academic, Social, and Emotional Learning, 2020), and evidence-based SEL programs are used in schools throughout Canada (Greenberg, Mahfouz, Davis, & Turksma, 2019). Now, teachers are often required to teach emotional literacy, including feelings words and self-regulation techniques as well as conflict resolution strategies (Collaborative for Academic, Social, and Emotional Learning, 2020). This shift acknowledges that emotions matter for all children and that creating a learning community that allows all children to thrive requires considering the whole child, not just the academic aspects of learning.

These SEL programs don't tend to include direct instruction and curricula around how to teach about race and racism. Instead, they tend to be a one-size-fits-all model. Students may learn what it means to be kind or inclusive but not how to understand differences and communicate across these differences with respect. Cultural competence, or the skills involved in enabling students to work effectively in cross-cultural situations, must be an essential part of our instruction if we hope to equip all students to be truly inclusive, antiracist members of society. In this sense, this teaching is not extra but a valuable part of our instruction.

In terms of where to find the time, it's helpful to approach this instruction the same way we approach other areas of instruction, by identifying learning goals and backward planning from there. This process allows us to integrate the teaching into existing units of study, rather than invent new units and add-ons. For example, if one of your goals is about showcasing how people of color have contributed to society in ways that have often gone under- or unappreciated, you can find the people you want to highlight in each area of study and integrate their stories and voices into these units. It's also helpful to critically examine all your teaching materials to ensure there are windows and mirrors for all your students, and, if you teach in a racially homogenous environment, ones that represent identities that exist outside of the classroom.

If you teach in a majority White environment, it's important to be intentional about decentralizing Whiteness so that your students gain a deep appreciation for the contributions and stories of non-White people. You can also integrate discussions about race and racism into social-emotional learning lessons, especially once you have defined terms with young students and allowed them to ask questions and aired any false ideas or misconceptions. Teaching about race and racism is about giving young students the tools to learn how to check their assumptions and work to form respectful, truly inclusive bonds with one another.

2. *How do I support students of color in these conversations?*

The first step for teachers is often to look inward, examine their fears about talking about race and racism, and grow their knowledge about their own racial identity (see appendix C, page 161, for a list of books).

Next, dedicate time at the beginning of the year to explore skin color differences, how skin color is different from race, and the dangers of excluding based on race, skin color, and other differences. This teaching will support all students, but especially students of color, when it's time to talk about Dr. King.

In addition, call out bias, ignorant statements, or microaggressions when they occur, and pay attention to the student impacted by these remarks, regardless of the intention of the person who committed them. The point is not to shame any individual student or to shut down conversations, but to let your students know the difference between impact and intent, and to teach the problem-solving skills all students need to repair damage when it's caused.

Finally, it's important for teachers to acknowledge their missteps and mistakes (such as failing to address bias when it occurs, giving incorrect information, or staying silent when you should have said something). In this way, teachers can model a growth mindset for students, letting them know that we all make mistakes, and that doesn't mean we are bad people.

3. *How do I respond to pushback from parents and caregivers?*

First, it's important to include families in the learning from day one, so that no one is caught off guard or surprised when their child comes home with new vocabulary and new information. Be explicit and honest about your teaching goals, and let parents and caregivers know why you are teaching this material. This could sound like,

> *I care deeply about creating a respectful and inclusive classroom community. Part of ensuring that each of my students is safe in my classroom and values their classmates is talking openly about all the ways*

we are the same and different from one another. This is the way we make sure we are not making assumptions about one another. In my classroom, we will discuss skin color, race, gender, and other pieces of identity, always with the goal of decreasing bias, increasing knowledge, and paying attention to what is developmentally appropriate for the age.

Offer specific examples of activities students will be engaging in throughout the year, such as art projects to help them find their skin color, or children's book titles you will be reading that explore issues of race and skin color. Make yourself available to answer any questions parents and caregivers have and stay focused on your goals for this instruction.

You can also provide research-based evidence around how young children notice differences at a younger age than some parents and caregivers realize, and the amount of bias that can go along with this noticing, if the developing biases aren't aired and corrected. For parents who don't feel competent in having these conversations at home, receiving guidance from teachers in the form of book suggestions or sample scripts can help grow competence. Pushback will most likely decrease the more proactive you are in providing information.

4. *How do I respond if I get pushback from administrators?*

First, find colleagues at your school who share your goals, who are equally dedicated to racial justice and antiracist practices. Whenever possible, handle pushback from administration collectively, with the support of colleagues.

Next, share research and best practices with school leaders who are doubtful about the value or relevance of this teaching. Share research that demonstrates that young students need help understanding differences so as not to form biases (Derman-Sparks & Edwards, 2020; Tatum, 2017; Winkler, 2009). Share the best practices you've learned around how to do this in the early childhood classrooms, such as identity-safe practices (Steele & Cohn-Vargas, 2013) or antibias practices (Derman-Sparks & Edwards, 2020). Describe the specific activities you're offering students and be explicit about your goals with these activities. It's helpful to conduct some informal pre- and post-assessments to demonstrate the real potential for this teaching to increase knowledge and decrease bias. For example, you could interview your students around where they think skin color comes from and what it means, document what they say, and ask the questions again after reading books about skin color.

If the pushback is around the conversation seeming too personal or more appropriate for the home environment, share research that shows the disparity between how often White families are engaging with their children about race as opposed to families of color (H. Stevenson, 2014). When I asked Andrew Grant-Thomas, cofounder of EmbraceRace, how to handle roadblocks and barriers that arise, he talked about the importance of community. He said,

> I think people who do this work in community, meaning that they can get support and feedback both in their own internal work and their work with their children, will be more engaged than those who don't have community in that work (A. Grant-Thomas, personal communication, March 2021).

If you get pushback from administrators about talking about race in the classroom, it's helpful to echo Grant-Thomas's idea, that the community approach, including teachers, family members, administration, and other members of the school community, is the most effective.

5. *How do I know what is developmentally appropriate for the age of the student?*

Young students will often let you know when your teaching is over their head. They begin to tune out or turn to their neighbor. When you ask for any questions or comments, there is an uncharacteristic silence. The opposite is also true. Young students will often let you know when they are passionate about something. When given the opportunity, they ask many questions about the world. Keep in mind as you determine when to introduce topics to students that very young children, aged two through six, haven't yet grasped abstract concepts and need lots of practice making the learning personal and meaningful (Common Sense Media, 2021). The best activities for younger learners are ones that engage their natural curiosity about the world around them.

This is the age to read books that celebrate all the different shades of skin color there are in the world (see appendix B, page 157, for a list of these books). As you read these books, it's also important to emphasize the importance and value of diversity. Preschoolers and kindergarteners should also engage in hands-on activities that allow them to further appreciate the diversity of skin tones, such as mixing paint to find their skin tones, and making artwork or writing poems about these colors. It's equally important to read picture books that give students a more scientific explanation of melanin, such as *All the Colors We Are* by Katie Kissinger (2014).

This is also the time to clear up any confusion your students may have about race. The earliest teachings about race are ones that provide a foundational understanding and allow young children to ask their questions and be curious about all the differences around them. But it's never too late for this kind of instruction. If an older student never learned the basics, it's OK to go back and teach these concepts.

When it comes to having more difficult conversations about racism, these conversations differ from one community to the next. What is considered developmentally appropriate for some may not be for others. One way to find out where to begin is to ask the parents and caregivers in your class how they approach the topic at home, and what their child already knows about racism. After you have a general sense of what your students know, define the terms you will be talking about with all your students so that everybody has shared knowledge.

No matter what age you teach, make sure to talk about how to be antiracist. Provide antiracist models of all races and ages, both famous and in your local community, both historic and currently working. Emphasizing hope and activism is a powerful way for children to see a path forward for themselves in social justice movements.

APPENDIX B

CHILDREN'S BOOKS THAT ADDRESS SKIN COLOR, RACE, HAIR, AND RELATED ISSUES

Consider the following resources and books to facilitate conversations with students about skin color, race, hair, and other identity-related topics. Remember it is important to have books featuring non-White characters doing everyday things, as well as books that explicitly discuss concepts like race and skin color.

Valuable Resources for Diversifying Classroom Libraries

- **"Building a Diverse, Anti-Bias Library for Young Children: A Masterpost" (https://bit.ly/3wKoYbB):** Early childhood educator Megan Pamela Ruth Madison's (2015) blog post is full of resources you can use to diversify your library and check out books for racism and sexism.
- **"Checklist: 8 Steps to Creating a Diverse Book Collection" (https://bit.ly/3n8IvPO):** Lee and Low Books (2014) created this checklist to help educators and parents create inclusive libraries for children.
- **Lee and Low Books (www.leeandlow.com):** Lee and Low Books is a multicultural book publisher, and includes books from grades preK–12, as well as some books for adults.
- **Teaching for Change (www.teachingforchange.org):** Teaching for Change offers a useful guide for selecting and rating antibias and social justice books for children, young adults, and educators that includes helpful guiding questions, including how many books are by and about people of color and Native Americans (Social Justice Books, 2017).

- **We Need Diverse Books (https://diversebooks.org):** This is a nonprofit dedicated to producing and promoting books that reflect the lives of all children.

Books That Address Skin Color

- *All the Colors of the Earth* by Sheila Hamanaka (1999)
- *All the Colors We Are: The Story of How We Get Our Skin Color* by Katie Kissinger (2014)
- *Brown Boy Joy* by Thomishia Booker (2018)
- *Brown Like Me* by Noelle Lamperti (2000)
- *I Am Enough* by Grace Byers (2018)
- *I Am Perfectly Designed* by Karamo Brown (2019)
- *Shades of Black: A Celebration of Our Children* by Sandra L. Pinkney (2006)
- *Shades of People* by Shelley Rotner and Sheila M. Kelly (2010)
- *Skin Again* by bell hooks (2017)
- *Sulwe* by Lupita Nyong'o (2019)
- *Tan to Tamarind: Poems About the Color Brown* by Malathi Michelle Iyengar (2009)
- *The Colors of Us* by Karen Katz (2002)
- *The Day You Begin* by Jacqueline Woodson (2018)
- *The Skin You Live In* by Michael Tyler (2005)

Books That Address Race

- *Antiracist Baby* by Ibram X. Kendi (2020)
- *Let's Talk About Race* by Julius Lester (2005)
- *Not My Idea: A Book About Whiteness* by Anastasia Higginbotham (2018)

Books That Address Hair

- *Big Hair, Don't Care* by Crystal Swain-Bates (2013)
- *Crown: An Ode to the Fresh Cut* by Derrick Barnes (2017)

- *Hair Dance!* by Dinah Johnson (2007)
- *Hair Like Mine* by LaTashia M. Perry (2015)
- *Hairs/Pelitos* by Sandra Cisneros (1997)
- *I Am Perfectly Designed* by Karamo Brown (2019)
- *I Love My Hair!* by Natasha Anastasia Tarpley (2001)
- *Pretty Brown Face* by Andrea and Brian Pinkney (1997)

Books That Address Similarities and Differences

- *Same, Same But Different* by Jenny Sue Kostecki-Shaw (2011)
- *We're Different, We're the Same* by Bobbi Jane Kates (1992)

Books That Address the Civil Rights Movement

- *A Sweet Smell of Roses* by Angela Johnson (2007)
- *Happy Birthday, Martin Luther King* by Jean Marzollo (2006)
- *Martin's Big Words: The Life of Dr. Martin Luther King, Jr.* by Doreen Rappaport (2001)
- *The Story of Martin Luther King Jr.* by Johnny Ray Moore (2015)
- *The Story of Ruby Bridges* by Robert Coles (2010)
- *The Youngest Marcher: The Story of Audrey Faye Hendricks, a Young Civil Rights Activist* by Cynthia Levinson (2017)
- *We March* by Shane W. Evans (2016)

Books That Address Changemakers

- *Isabel's House of Butterflies* by Tony Johnston (2005)
- *Luna and Me: The True Story of a Girl Who Lived in a Tree to Save a Forest* by Jenny Sue Kostecki-Shaw (2015)
- *Mama Miti: Wangari Maathai and the Trees of Kenya* by Donna Jo Napoli (2010)
- *Seeds of Change: Wangari's Gift to the World* by Jen Cullerton Johnson (2010)

- *The Power of Her Pen: The Story of Groundbreaking Journalist Ethel L. Payne* by Lesa Cline-Ransome (2020)
- *Wangari's Trees of Peace: A True Story From Africa* by Jeanette Winter (2018)

APPENDIX C

BOOKS FOR ADULTS ON RACE AND RACISM

For teachers who are new to learning about race and racism, it can be overwhelming to find a starting point. Consider the following books to support your learning. These can also be helpful resources when a student, family member, or colleague asks a question you are not sure how to answer.

Books That Address the History of the Civil Rights Movement

- *At Canaan's Edge: America in the King Years, 1965–68* by Taylor Branch (2007)
- *Parting the Waters: America in the King Years, 1954–63* by Taylor Branch (1989)
- *Pillar of Fire: America in the King Years, 1963–65* by Taylor Branch (1998)

Books That Address Systemic Racism

- *Between the World and Me* by Ta-Nehisi Coates (2015)
- *Caste: The Origins of Our Discontents* by Isabel Wilkerson (2020)
- *How to Be an Antiracist* by Ibram X. Kendi (2019)
- *Just Mercy: A Story of Justice and Redemption* by Bryan Stevenson (2014)
- *The Cross of Redemption: Uncollected Writings* by James Baldwin (2010)
- *The New Jim Crow: Mass Incarceration in the Age of Colorblindness* by Michelle Alexander (2010)

Books That Address Whiteness

- *Dear White America: Letter to a New Minority* by Tim Wise (2012)
- *White Like Me: Reflections on Race from a Privileged Son* by Tim Wise (2011)
- *Witnessing Whiteness: The Need to Talk About Race and How to Do It* by Shelly Tochluk (2010)

Books That Address Antibias and Identity-Safe Practices

- *Anti-Bias Education for Young Children and Ourselves* by Louise Derman-Sparks and Julie Olsen Edwards (2020)
- *Identity Safe Classrooms, Grades K–5: Places to Belong and Learn* by Dorothy M. Steele and Becki Cohn-Vargas (2013)
- *What If All the Kids Are White? Anti-Bias Multicultural Education with Young Children and Families* by Louise Derman-Sparks and Patricia G. Ramsey (2011)
- *Whistling Vivaldi: How Stereotypes Affect Us and What We Can Do* by Claude M. Steele (2011)

REFERENCES AND RESOURCES

Abaied, J. L., & Perry, S. P. (2021). Socialization of racial ideology by White parents. *Cultural Diversity and Ethnic Minority Psychology, 27*(3), 431–440.

Aboud, F. E. (2008). A social-cognitive developmental theory of prejudice. In S. M. Quintana & C. McKown (Eds.), *Handbook of race, racism, and the developing child* (pp. 55–71). Hoboken, NJ: John Wiley & Sons.

Adams, A. (Summer 2014). Four roads converge. *Independent School Magazine*, 40–47. Accessed at https://aladamsdotorg.files.wordpress.com/2016/02/four-roads-article.pdf on January 31, 2022.

Alexander, M. (2010). *The new Jim Crow: Mass incarceration in the age of colorblindness.* New York: New Press.

American RadioWorks. (n.d.). *Robert P. Moses.* Accessed at http://americanradioworks.publicradio.org/features/blackspeech/bmoses.html on August 4, 2021.

Anderson, R. E., & Brown, C. S. (2019). It's never too young to talk about race and gender. *Human Development, 63*(1–3). Accessed at DOI: 10.1159/000501242 on July 30, 2021.

Anderson, R. E., & Stevenson, H. C. (2019). RECASTing racial stress and trauma: Theorizing the healing potential of racial socialization in families. *American Psychologist, 74*(1), 63–75.

Asare, J. G. (2020, January 8). Stop asking Black people if you can touch their hair. *Forbes.* Accessed at www.forbes.com/sites/janicegassam/2020/01/08/stop-asking-black-people-if-you-can-touch-their-hair/?sh=21d0c29050a7 on December 8, 2021.

Baldwin, J. (2010). *The cross of redemption: Uncollected writings.* New York: Pantheon Books.

Barnes, D. (2017). *Crown: An ode to the fresh cut.* Evanston, IL: Agate Bolden.

Barney, L. (2020, December 16). *Diversity of S&P 500 boards continues to improve.* Accessed at www.planadviser.com/diversity-sp-500-boards-continues-improve on January 31, 2022.

Bartoli, E., Michael, A., Bentley-Edwards, K. L., Stevenson, H. C., Shor, R. F., & McClain, S. E. (2016). Training for colour-blindness: White racial socialization. *Whiteness and Education, 1*(2), 125–136.

Beauvais, G., & Jones, S. A. (2013). *I am mixed.* North Hollywood, CA: Stranger Comics.

Bishop, R. S. (1990). Mirrors, windows, and sliding glass doors. *Perspectives, 1*(3), ix–xi.

Black Lives Matter. (n.d.). *About.* Accessed at https://blacklivesmatter.com/about/ on February 28, 2022.

Blan, L., & Cimpian, A. (2017). Gender stereotypes about intellectual ability emerge early and influence children's interests. *Science, 355*(6323), 389–391. Accessed at https://science.sciencemag.org/content/355/6323/389 on July 30, 2021.

BLM at School. (n.d.). Black Lives Matter *at school.* Accessed at blacklivesmatteratschool.com on August 5, 2021.

Block, M. (2020, October 30). *Agencies, contractors suspend diversity training to avoid violating Trump order.* Accessed at www.npr.org/2020/10/30/929165869/agencies-contractors-suspend-diversity-training-to-avoid-violating-trump-order on December 6, 2021.

Booker, T. (2018). *Brown boy joy.* Scotts Valley, CA: CreateSpace.

Borger, J. (2021). MAGA vs. BLM: How police handled the Capitol mob and George Floyd activists—in pictures. *The Guardian.* Accessed at www.theguardian.com/us-news/2021/jan/06/capitol-mob-police-trump-george-floyd-protests-photos on July 30, 2021.

Bose, N., & Brice, M. (2021). *If rioters were Black, "hundreds" would have been killed: Washington reflects on Capitol rampage.* Accessed at www.reuters.com/article/us-usa-election-inequality/if-rioters-were-black-hundreds-would-have-been-killed-washington-reflects-on-capitol-rampage-idUSKBN29D1HM on July 30, 2021.

Branch, T. (1989). *Parting the waters: America in the King years, 1954–63.* New York: Simon & Schuster.

Branch, T. (1998). *Pillar of fire: America in the King years, 1963–65.* New York: Simon & Schuster.

Branch, T. (2007). *At Canaan's edge: America in the King years, 1965–68.* New York: Simon & Schuster.

Bronson, P., & Merryman, A. (2009). *NurtureShock: New thinking about children.* New York: Hachette Book Group.

Brown, A. C. (2019). Engaging and embracing Black parents. In L. Delpit (Ed.), *Teaching when the world is on fire: Authentic classroom advice, from climate justice to Black Lives Matter* (pp. 119–127). New York: New Press.

Brown, K. (2019). *I am perfectly designed.* New York: Henry Holt & Co.

Brown v. Board of Education of Topeka, 347 U.S. 483 (1954).

Buchanan, L., Bui, Q., & Patel, J. K. (2020, July 3). Black Lives Matter may be the largest movement in U.S. History. *The New York Times.* Accessed at www.nytimes.com/interactive/2020/07/03/us/george-floyd-protests-crowd-size.html on December 8, 2021.

Bullard, L. (2015). *My family, your family.* Minneapolis, MN: Millbrook Press.

Byers, G. (2018). *I am enough.* New York: Balzer + Bray.

Carson, E. A. (2018). *Prisoners in 2016.* Accessed at https://bjs.ojp.gov/library/publications/prisoners-2016 on August 6, 2021.

Cartledge, G., Yurick, A. L., & Telesman, A. O. (2022). *There's more to the story.* Bloomington, IN: Solution Tree Press.

Cashin, S. (2017). *Loving: Interracial intimacy in America and the threat to White supremacy.* Boston: Beacon Press.

Caven, M. (2020, July 27). *Why we need an anti-racist approach to social and emotional learning* [Blog post]. Accessed at www.edc.org/blog/why-we-need-anti-racist-approach-social-and-emotional-learning on August 6, 2021.

Champion, D., & Grant, S. (2008). *The spirit of the baobab tree.* Bloomington, IN: Xlibris.

Changing the Face of Medicine. (n.d.). *Dr. Patricia E. Bath.* Accessed at https://cfmedicine.nlm.nih.gov/physicians/biography_26.html on December 13, 2021.

Charter for Compassion. (n.d.). *Ruler is a Charter for Compassion partner.* Accessed at https://charterforcompassion.org/yale-center-for-emotional-intelligence on February 28, 2022.

Chavez, L., & Frankenberg, E. (2009). *Integration defended: Berkeley Unified's strategy to maintain school diversity.* Accessed at https://civilrightsproject.ucla.edu/research/k-12-education/integration-and-diversity/integration-defended-berkeley-unified2019s-strategy-to-maintain-school-diversity on August 6, 2021.

Cisneros, S. (1997). *Hairs / Pelitos.* New York: Dragonfly Books.

City of Berkeley. (2017, July 25). *Berkeley homeless point-in-time count and survey data.* Accessed at www.cityofberkeley.info/Clerk/City_Council/2017/07_Jul/Documents/2017-07-25_Item_53_2017_Berkeley_Homeless.aspx on December 10, 2021.

The Civil Rights Project. (n.d.). *Resources on major court decisions.* Accessed at https://civilrightsproject.ucla.edu/legal-developments/court-decisions/ on August 6, 2021.

Cline-Ransome, L. (2020). *The power of her pen: The story of groundbreaking journalist Ethel L. Payne.* New York: Simon & Schuster.

CNN. (2010, May 14). *Study: White and black children biased toward lighter skin.* Accessed at www.cnn.com/2010/US/05/13/doll.study/index.html on November 8, 2021.

Coates, T. (2015). *Between the world and me.* Melbourne, Victoria, Australia: Text Publishing Co.

Coates, T. (2017). *We were eight years in power: An American tragedy.* New York: Penguin Random House.

Cohn-Vargas, B. (2012, April 24). *Trayvon Martin: The wakeup call to end stereotype threat* [Blog post]. Accessed at www.edutopia.org/blog/stereotype-threat-identity-safety-becki-cohn-vargas on October 20, 2021.

Coles, R. (2010). *The story of Ruby Bridges.* New York: Scholastic.

Collaborative for Academic, Social, and Emotional Learning. (2020, March 1). *An examination of K–12 SEL learning competencies and standards in 18 states.* Accessed at https://casel.org/casel-gateway-examining-kthru12-learning-competencies on January 31, 2022.

Collins, C. (2018, Fall). What is White privilege, really? *Learning for Justice, 60.* Accessed at www.learningforjustice.org/magazine/fall-2018/what-is-white-privilege-really on August 6, 2021.

Collins, J., Dias, M., Harmon, D., Hyman, F., Sisson-Talbert, L., & Talbert, D. E. (Executive Producers). (2020). *Bookmarks: Celebrating Black voices* [Television series]. Los Gatos, CA: Netflix.

Common Sense Media. (2021, April 21). *How to talk about difficult topics with your children: An age-by-age guide.* Accessed at www.mother.ly/life/how-to-talk-to-your-kids-about-difficult-world-eventsby-age on January 31, 2022.

Cooperative Children's Book Center. (2020, June 16). *The numbers are in: 2019 CCBC statistics.* Accessed at https://ccbc.education.wisc.edu/the-numbers-are-in-2019-ccbc-diversity-statistics/ on November 29, 2021.

Delmont, M. (2019, July 1). There's a generational shift in the debate over busing. *The Atlantic.* Accessed at www.theatlantic.com/ideas/archive/2019/07/kamala-harris-and-busing-debate/593047/ on August 6, 2021.

Delpit, L. (2006). *Other people's children: Cultural conflict in the classroom* (2nd ed.). New York: New Press.

Derman-Sparks, L., & Edwards, J. O. (2010). *Anti-bias education for young children and ourselves* (2nd ed.). Washington, DC: National Association for the Education of Young Children.

Derman-Sparks, L., & Edwards, J. O. (2020). *Anti-bias education for young children and ourselves* (Rev. 2nd ed.). Washington, DC: National Association for the Education of Young Children.

Derman-Sparks, L., & Ramsey, P. G. (2011). *What if all the kids are White? Anti-bias multicultural education with young children and families* (2nd ed.). New York: Teacher's College Press.

Devos, T., & Banaji, M. R. (2005). America = White? *Journal of Personality and Social Psychology, 88*(3), 447–466.

Dewan, S., MacFarquhar, N., Kanno-Youngs, Z., & Watkins, A. (2021, January 7). Police failures spur resignations and complaints of double standards. *The New York Times.* Accessed at www.nytimes.com/2021/01/07/us/Capitol-cops-police.html on August 6, 2021.

DiAngelo, R. (2012). Nothing to add: A challenge to White silence in racial discussions. *Understanding and Dismantling Privilege, 2*(1), 2–17. Accessed at www.wpcjournal.com/article/view/10100 on August 6, 2021.

Dias, M. (n.d.). *About me.* Accessed at www.marleydias.com/about/ on February 28, 2022.

Diaz, J. (2021, October 20). *Teachers and civil rights groups sue over Oklahoma's ban on critical race theory.* Accessed at www.npr.org/2021/10/20/1047519861/aclu-sues-over-oklahoma-law-on-critical-race-theory on February 28, 2022.

Dr. Seuss. (1971). *The Lorax.* New York: Random House.

Dusenbury, L. (2018, August). States are stepping up to support social and emotional learning. *Education Week.* Accessed at www.edweek.org/education/opinion-states-are-stepping-up-to-support-social-and-emotional-learning/2018/08 on August 6, 2021.

Dweck, C. (2014, November). *The power of believing that you can improve* [Video file]. Accessed at www.ted.com/talks/carol_dweck_the_power_of_believing_that_you_can_improve on August 6, 2021.

Dweck, C. (2015, September 22). Carol Dweck revisits the "growth mindset." *Education Week.* Accessed at www.edweek.org/ew/articles/2015/09/23/carol-dweck-revisits-the-growth-mindset.html on August 6, 2021.

Dweck, C. (2017). *Mindset: The new psychology of success* (Updated ed.). New York: Penguin Random House.

EdBrief. (2019, March 9). *Despite federal retreat from supporting school diversity, some districts forge ahead with school designs for integration.* Accessed at www.edbrief.com/Archives/govLead/govLead190309_despiteFederal.php on October 18, 2021.

Ellis, R. (2021, January 6). *Portland's protestors spot double standard in restrained response to Capitol insurrection.* Accessed at www.opb.org/article/2021/01/06/portland-oregon-protest-capitol-washington/ on August 6, 2021.

EmbraceRace, & MomsRising. (n.d.). *10 tips for teaching and talking to kids about race.* Accessed at www.embracerace.org/resources/teaching-and-talking-to-kids on August 6, 2021.

Evans, S. W. (2016). *We march.* New York: Square Fish.

Frankenberg, E., & Orfield, G. (Eds.). (2007). *Lessons in integration: Realizing the promise of racial diversity in America's schools.* Charlottesville: University of Virginia Press.

Freedberg, L. (2019, July 5). *Fifty years after desegregation, wide racial and ethnic achievement gaps persist in Berkeley.* Accessed at https://edsource.org/2019/fifty-years-after-desegregation-wide-racial-and-ethnic-achievement-gaps-persist-in-berkeley/614645 on August 6, 2021.

Freire, P. (2000). *Pedagogy of the oppressed* (M.B. Ramos Trans., 30th anniversary ed.). New York: Continuum.

Fusion Comedy. (2016, October 5). *How microaggressions are like mosquito bites* [Video file]. Accessed at www.youtube.com/watch?v=hDd3bzA7450 on August 4, 2021.

Gardner, H. (2006). *Five minds for the future.* Boston: Harvard Business Review Press.

Genhart, M. (2015). *Ouch! moments: When words are used in hurtful ways.* Washington, DC: Magination Press.

Gleibermann, E. (2017, June 1). The college-town achievement gap. *The Atlantic.* Accessed at www.theatlantic.com/education/archive/2017/06/the-college-town-achievement-gap/526305/ on August 6, 2021.

Gonzalez, J. (2017, September 10). *Culturally responsive teaching: 4 misconceptions.* Accessed at www.cultofpedagogy.com/culturally-responsive-misconceptions on August 6, 2021.

Greenberg, M. T., Mahfouz, J., Davis, M., & Turksma, C. (2019, December 4). *Social emotional learning for principals.* Accessed at www.edcan.ca/articles/sel-for-principals on January 31, 2022.

The Green Belt Movement. (n.d.). *Be a hummingbird.* Accessed at www.greenbeltmovement.org/get-involved/be-a-hummingbird on August 5, 2021.

Greene, R. W. (2014). *Lost at school: Why our kids with behavioral challenges are falling through the cracks and how we can help them.* New York: Scribner.

Gulati-Partee, G., & Potapchuk, M. (2014). Paying attention to White culture and privilege: A missing link to advancing racial equity. *The Foundation Review, 6*(1), 25–38. Accessed at www.mpassociates.us/uploads/3/7/1/0/37103967/paying_attention_to_white_culture_and_privilege-_a_missi.pdf on August 6, 2021.

Guynn, J. (2021a, January 6). "Burn down DC": Violence that erupted at Capitol was incited by pro-Trump mob on social media. *USA Today*. Accessed at www.usatoday.com/story/tech/2021/01/06/trump-riot-twitter-parler-proud-boys-boogaloos-antifa-qanon/6570794002/ on August 6, 2021.

Guynn, J. (2021b, January 8). Donald Trump executive order banning diversity training suspended by Labor Department. *USA Today*. Accessed at www.usatoday.com/story/money/2021/01/07/trump-diversity-training-ban-labor-department-suspends-executive-order/6586373002/ on November 15, 2021.

Haberman, M. (2021, January 6). Trump told crowd "You will never take back our country with weakness." *The New York Times*. Accessed at www.nytimes.com/2021/01/06/us/politics/trump-speech-capitol.html on August 6, 2021.

Hamanaka, S. (1999). *All the colors of the Earth*. New York: HarperCollins.

Hammond, Z. (2015a, April 1). *3 tips to make any lesson more culturally responsive*. Accessed at www.cultofpedagogy.com/culturally-responsive-teaching-strategies on August 6, 2021.

Hammond, Z. (2015b). *Culturally responsive teaching and the brain: Promoting authentic engagement and rigor among culturally and linguistically diverse students*. Thousand Oaks, CA: Corwin Press.

hannahehrlich. (2014). *Checklist: 8 steps to creating a diverse book collection* [Blog post]. Accessed at https://blog.leeandlow.com/2014/05/22/checklist-8-steps-to-creating-a-diverse-book-collection/ on August 5, 2021.

Hannah-Jones, N. (2016, November 15). The end of the postracial myth. *The New York Times Magazine*. Accessed at www.nytimes.com/interactive/2016/11/20/magazine/donald-trumps-america-iowa-race.html on November 1, 2021.

Henderson, A. T., & Mapp, K. L. (2002). *A new wave of evidence: The impact of school, family, and community connections on student achievement*. Austin, TX: National Center for Family and Community Connections with Schools.

Higginbotham, A. (2018). *Not my idea: A book about whiteness*. New York: Dottir Press.

Hirschfeld, L. A. (2012). Seven myths of race and the young child. *Du Bois Review Social Science Research on Race, 9*(1).

Hoexter, T. (2015). *A wrinkled heart* [E-reader version]. Accessed at http://bookprem.com/gd-ebooks/B014X65DQM on November 29, 2021.

Hofstaedter, M. (n.d.). *Claudette Colvin—A brave advocate for racial equality*. Accessed at https://inspiremykids.com/claudette-colvin-a-brave-advocate-for-racial-equality/ on August 4, 2021.

hooks, b. (2017). *Skin again*. Boston: Little, Brown.

Huyck, D., & Dahlen, S. P. (2019). *Picture this: Diversity in children's books, 2018 infographic.* Accessed at https://readingspark.wordpress.com/2019/06/19/picture-this-diversity-in-childrens-books-2018-infographic/readingspark.wordpress.com on August 6, 2021.

Ibiblio. (n.d.a). *Ella Baker.* Accessed at www.ibiblio.org/sncc/baker.html on August 5, 2021.

Ibiblio. (n.d.b). *John Lewis.* Accessed at www.ibiblio.org/sncc/lewis.html on August 4, 2021.

Infoplease. (n.d.). *Bayard Rustin biography.* Accessed at www.infoplease.com/ipa/A0900070.html on August 4, 2021.

Ishizuka, K., & Stephens, R. (2019). The cat is out of the bag: Orientalism, anti-Blackness, and White supremacy in Dr. Seuss's children's books. *Research on Diversity in Youth Literature, 1*(2), Article 4.

Ishmael, S., & Tunstall, J. (2019). The fire. In L. Delpit (Ed.), *Teaching when the world is on fire: Authentic classroom advice, from climate justice to Black Lives Matter* (pp. 108–118). New York: New Press.

Iyengar, M. M. (2009). *Tan to tamarind: Poems about the color brown.* San Francisco: Children's Book Press.

Johnson, A. (2007). *A sweet smell of roses.* New York: Simon & Schuster.

Johnson, D. (2007). *Hair dance!* New York: Henry Holt & Co.

Johnson, J. C. (2010). *Seeds of change: Wangari's gift to the world.* New York: Lee and Low Books.

Johnson, R. C. (2011). *Long-run impacts of school desegregation & school quality on adult attainments* [Working Paper No. 16664]. Cambridge, MA: National Bureau of Economic Research. Accessed at www.nber.org/papers/w16664 on August 6, 2021.

Johnston, T. (2005). *Isabel's house of butterflies.* San Francisco: Sierra Club Books.

Jones, E., & Reynolds, G. (2011). *The play's the thing: Teachers' roles in children's play.* (2nd ed.). New York: Teachers College Press.

Jones, S. (2020, February 18). *Inclusive leadership* [Video file]. Accessed at www.youtube.com/watch?v=AYwUww2aWBY on January 31, 2022.

Kamenetz, A. (2016, February 29). *When integrating a school, does it matter if you use class instead of race?* Accessed at www.npr.org/sections/ed/2016/02/29/466543209/when-integrating-a-school-does-it-matter-if-you-use-class-instead-of-race on August 6, 2021.

Kanno-Youngs, Z., Tavernise, S., & Cochrane, E. (2021, January 6). As House was breached, a fear "we'd have to fight" to get out. *The New York Times.* Accessed at www.nytimes.com/2021/01/06/us/politics/capitol-breach-trump-protests.html on August 6, 2021.

Kates, B. J. (1992). *We're different, we're the same.* New York: Random House.

Katz, K. (2002). *The colors of us.* New York: Square Fish.

Kelm, N. (2021, April 22). *Researchers ask: How do white parents talk about race?* Accessed at www.uvm.edu/news/story/researchers-ask-how-do-white-parents-talk-about-race on January 31, 2022.

Kendall, F. E. (2013). *Understanding White privilege: Creating pathways to authentic relationships across race* (2nd ed.). New York: Routledge.

Kendi, I. X. (2019). *How to be an antiracist.* New York: One World.

Kendi, I. X. (2020). *Antiracist baby.* New York: Kokila.

The Kennedy Center. (n.d.). *Alvin Ailey + Revelations.* Accessed at www.kennedy-center.org/education/resources-for-educators/classroom-resources/media-and-interactives/media/dance/alvin-ailey—revelations/ on December 13, 2021.

Kirwan Institute for the Study of Race and Ethnicity. (2012, May 29). *Understanding implicit bias.* Accessed at https://kirwaninstitute.osu.edu/article/understanding-implicit-bias on August 4, 2021.

Kissinger, K. (2014). *All the colors we are: The story of how we get our skin color.* St. Paul, MN: Redleaf Press.

Kivel, P. (2017). *Uprooting racism: How White people can work for racial justice* (4th ed.). Gabriola Island, British Columbia, Canada: New Society Press.

Kostecki-Shaw, J. S. (2011). *Same, same but different.* New York: Henry Holt & Co.

Kostecki-Shaw, J. S. (2015). *Luna & me: The true story of a girl who lived in a tree to save a forest.* New York: Henry Holt & Co.

Kramer, A. (2016, November 10). Claude Steele explains stereotype threat. *The Brown Daily Herald.* Accessed at www.browndailyherald.com/2016/11/10/professor-explains-stereotype-threat/ on August 6, 2021.

Lamperti, N. (2000). *Brown like me.* Lebanon, NH: Dingman / McKay.

Lattimore, K. (2017, July 17). *When Black hair violates the dress code.* Accessed at www.npr.org/sections/ed/2017/07/17/534448313/when-black-hair-violates-the-dress-code on August 6, 2021.

LDF Director-Counsels. (n.d.). *Thurgood Marshall.* Accessed at www.naacpldf.org/about-us/history/thurgood-marshall/ on August 4, 2021.

Learning for Justice. (n.d.a). *Art and activism.* Accessed at www.learningforjustice.org/classroom-resources/lessons/art-and-activism on August 4, 2021.

Learning for Justice. (n.d.b). *Cross-racial understanding and reduction of racial prejudice.* Accessed at www.learningforjustice.org/professional-development/crossracial-understanding-and-reduction-of-racial-prejudice on December 10, 2021.

Learning for Justice. (n.d.c). *White anti-racist biographies: Early grades.* Accessed at www.learningforjustice.org/classroom-resources/lessons/white-antiracist-biographies-early-grades on August 4, 2021.

Learning for Justice. (n.d.d). *Who has hair?* Accessed at www.learningforjustice.org/classroom-resources/lessons/who-has-hair on August 4, 2021.

Lee, E., Menkart, D., & Okazawa-Rey, M. (2002). *Beyond heroes & holidays: A practical guide to K–12 anti-racist, multicultural education and staff development.* Washington, DC: Teaching for Change.

Lee, M. Y. H. (2015, July 7). Yes, U.S. locks people up at a higher rate than any other country. *The Washington Post.* Accessed at http://washingtonpost.com/news/fact-checker/wp/2015/07/07/yes-u-s-locks-people-up-at-a-higher-rate-than-any-other-country on January 31, 2022.

Lee, R. E. R. (2015, August 31). *What's missing from the conversation: The growth mindset in cultural competency.* Accessed at www.nais.org/learn/independent-ideas/august-2015/what%E2%80%99s-missing-from-the-conversation-the-growth-m/ on August 6, 2021.

Lee, R. E. R. (2018). *Old school diversity to 21st century cultural competency* [Slideware presentation]. Accessed at www.slideshare.net/leerosetta/nais-pocc-2018-cultural-competency on August 6, 2021.

Lee and Low Books. (2014). *Checklist: 8 steps to creating a diverse book collection.* Accessed at https://blog.leeandlow.com/2014/05/22/checklist-8-steps-to-creating-a-diverse-book-collection/ on March 21, 2022.

Lester, J. (2005). *Let's talk about race.* New York: HarperCollins.

Levinson, C. (2017). *The youngest marcher: The story of Audrey Faye Hendricks, a young civil rights activist.* New York: Atheneum.

Liptak, A. (2013, June 25). Supreme court invalidates key part of Voting Rights Act. *The New York Times.* Accessed at www.nytimes.com/2013/06/26/us/supreme-court-ruling.html on February 28, 2022.

Local Government Commission. (n.d.). *Improving police and community relations.* Accessed at www.lgc.org/newsletter/jul2016 on August 9, 2021.

Lowman, E. M., & Barker, A. (n.d.). *Deloria Jr, Vine.* Accessed at https://globalsocialtheory.org/thinkers/vine-deloria-jr/ on August 5, 2021.

Madison, M. P. R. (2015, August 12). *Building a diverse, anti-bias library for young children: A masterpost.* Accessed at https://earlychildhoodequity.tumblr.com/post/126556770455/building-a-diverse-anti-bias-library-for-young on August 6, 2021.

Mapp, K. L., Henderson, A. T., & Hill, N. E. (2014, May 15). *Does family engagement matter? The truth and half-truths about parent involvement.* Accessed at www.teachingforchange.org/does-family-engagement-matter on August 6, 2021.

Marzollo, J. (2006). *Happy birthday, Martin Luther King.* New York: Scholastic.

Masurel, C. (2003). *Two homes.* Somerville, MA: Candlewick Press.

McCoy, T. (2014, November 25). Darren Wilson explains why he killed Michael Brown. *The Washington Post.* Accessed at www.washingtonpost.com/news/morning-mix/wp/2014/11/25/why-darren-wilson-said-he-killed-michael-brown/ on August 6, 2021.

McGrath, M. (2017, June 13). From activist to author: How 12-year-old Marley Dias is changing the face of children's literature. *Forbes.* Accessed at www.forbes.com/sites/maggiemcgrath/2017/06/13/from-activist-to-author-how-12-year-old-marley-dias-is-changing-the-face-of-childrens-literature/?sh=45aa4b6a4ce0 on August 6, 2021.

McIntosh, P. (1988). *White privilege and male privilege: A personal account of coming to see correspondences through work in women's studies.* Accessed at www.wcwonline.org/images/pdf/White_Privilege_and_Male_Privilege_Personal_Account-Peggy_McIntosh.pdf on August 6, 2021.

McNair, J. C., & Edwards, P. A. (2021, June 28). The lasting legacy of Rudine Sims Bishop: Mirrors, windows, sliding glass doors, and more. *Literacy Research: Theory, Method, and Practice, 70*(1), 202–212.

Michael, A., & Bartoli, E. (2014). *What White children need to know about race.* Accessed at www.nais.org/magazine/independent-school/summer-2014/what-white-children-need-to-know-about-race/ on August 6, 2021.

Milliarium Zero. (2011). *Myles Horton.* Accessed at www.yougottomove.com/myles.html on August 5, 2021.

Milligan, S. (2021, January 6). Trump calls election fraudulent, tells supporters to go home. *U.S. News & World Report.* Accessed at www.usnews.com/news/elections/articles/2021-01-06/trump-calls-election-fraudulent-tells-supporters-to-go-home on August 6, 2021.

Mirrorswindowsdoors.org. (2015, April 8). *The life of trees and the tree of life: An annotated list of multicultural non-fiction picture books about tree.* Accessed at shttp://mirrorswindowsdoors.org/wp/picture-books-trees-nonfiction/ on August 5, 2021.

Mohdin, A. (2020, November 19). Gladys West: The hidden figure who helped invent GPS. *The Guardian.* Accessed at www.theguardian.com/society/2020/nov/19/gladys-west-the-hidden-figure-who-helped-invent-gps on December 13, 2021.

Moore, J. R. (2015). *The story of Martin Luther King Jr.* New York: WorthyKids.

Murse, T. (2020). *What is gerrymandering?* Accessed at www.thoughtco.com/what-is-gerrymandering-4057603 on August 6, 2021.

NAACP. (n.d.). *Julian Bond.* Accessed at https://naacp.org/find-resources/history-explained/civil-rights-leaders/julian-bond on August 4, 2021.

NAACP Legal Defense and Educational Fund. (n.d.). *A revealing experiment: Brown v. Board and "The Doll Test."* Accessed at www.naacpldf.org/ldf-celebrates-60th-anniversary-brown-v-board-education/significance-doll-test/ on November 8, 2021.

Napoli, D. J. (2010). *Mama Miti: Wangari Maathai and the trees of Kenya.* New York: Simon & Schuster.

National Education Association. (n.d.). *Black Lives Matter at school—Resources.* Accessed at https://neaedjustice.org/black-lives-matter-school-resources/ on August 5, 2021.

Natkin, S. B. (2013). *Growing character: Raising culturally aware children.* Accessed at www.parentmap.com/article/growing-character-raising-culturally-aware-children on March 14, 2022.

Nguyen A. (2021). "Children have the fairest things to say": Young children's engagement with antibias picture books. *Early Childhood Education Journal*, 1–17.

Nobel Prize. (n.d.). *Wangari Maathai.* Accessed at www.nobelprize.org/prizes/peace/2004/maathai/facts/ on December 17, 2021.

Nottingham, J. (2017). *The learning challenge: How to guide your students through the learning pit to achieve deeper understanding.* Thousand Oaks, CA: SAGE.

Nyong'o, L. (2019). *Sulwe.* New York: Simon & Schuster.

Orfield, G., Kucsera, J., & Siegel-Hawley, G. (2012). *E pluribus…separation: Deepening double segregation for more students.* Los Angeles: The Civil Rights Project at UCLA.

Oluo, I. (2018). *So you want to talk about race.* New York: Hachette Book Group.

PA Upload. (2021, January 12). *The color of me* [Video file]. Accessed at www.youtube.com/watch?v=uFIdGUmBD8Q on August 9, 2021.

Parents Involved in Community Schools v. Seattle School District No. 1, 551 U.S. 701 (2007).

Parker, K., Williams, A., & Steele, J. R. (2015). Children's racial categorization in context. *Child Development Perspective, 10*(1), 33–38. Accessed at https://srcd.onlinelibrary.wiley.com/doi/10.1111/cdep.12155 on December 26, 2021.

Parr, T. (2003). *The family book.* New York: Little, Brown.

Peck, R. (Director). (2016). *I am not your negro* [Documentary]. United States: Magnolia Pictures.

Perry, L. M. (2015). *Hair like mine.* Detroit, MI: G Publishing.

Phillips, K. (2014, September 19). *Diversity and inclusion for all: Understanding the intersection of multiple characteristics* [Slideware presentation]. Accessed at https://issuu.com/bernsteincenter/docs/diversityinc.final on August 6, 2021.

Pinkney, A., & Pinkney, B. (1997). *Pretty brown face.* Boston: Clarion.

Pinkney, S. L. (2006). *Shades of Black: A celebration of our children.* New York: Cartwheel Books.

Potok, M. (2017). The year in hate and extremism. *The Intelligence Report.* Accessed at www.splcenter.org/intelligence-report?f%5B0%5D=field_intel_report_issue%3A12053 on December 8, 2021.

Proctor & Gamble. (2020, June 2). *The talk* [Video file]. Accessed at www.youtube.com/watch?v=XPl3hZqFaLM on August 3, 2021.

Quintana, S. M., & McKown, C. (2008). *Handbook of race, racism, and the developing child.* San Francisco: John Wiley & Sons.

Racial Equity Tools. (2020). *Racial equity tools glossary.* Accessed at www.racialequitytools.org/glossary on March 14, 2022.

Rappaport, D. (2001). *Martin's big words: The life of Dr. Martin Luther King, Jr.* Boston: Little, Brown.

Régner, I., Steele, J., & Huguet, P. (2014). Stereotype threat in children: Past and present. *International Review of Social Psychology, 27*(3), 5–12. Accessed at www.researchgate.net/publication/279321357_Stereotype_threat_in_children_Past_and_present on August 6, 2021.

Richardson, J., & Parnell, P. (2015). *And Tango makes three.* New York: Little Simon.

Roediger, D. (n.d.). *Historical foundations of race.* Accessed at https://nmaahc.si.edu/learn/talking-about-race/topics/historical-foundations-race on December 6, 2021.

Rogin, M. (n.d.). *What I can do as a White mom after Darren Wilson's acquittal. InCultureParent.* Accessed at www.incultureparent.com/what-i-can-do-as-a-white-mom-after-darren-wilsons-acquittal/ on October 27, 2021.

Rogin, M. (2013). How to talk to kindergarteners about race. *InCultureParent.* Accessed at www.incultureparent.com/how-i-talk-to-my-kindergarten-classroom-about-race/ on October 8, 2021.

Rotner, S., & Kelly, S. M. (2010). *Shades of people.* New York: Holiday House.

Safi, M. (2020, June 9). George Floyd killing triggers wave of activism around the world. *The Guardian.* Accessed at www.theguardian.com/us-news/2020/jun/09/george-floyd-killing-triggers-wave-of-activism-around-the-world on March 14, 2022.

Sanders, T. (2016, October 16). "Only White people," said the little girl. *The New York Times*. Accessed at www.nytimes.com/2016/10/16/opinion/sunday/only-white-people-said-the-little-girl.html on August 6, 2021.

Schaffer, A. (2017, December 19). The remarkable career of Shirley Ann Jackson. *MIT Technology Review*. Accessed at www.technologyreview.com/2017/12/19/146775/the-remarkable-career-of-shirley-ann-jackson/ on December 13, 2021.

Schoinas, E. (2020, August 20). *#1000BlackGirlBooks: A push for representation in children's literature*. Accessed at https://msmagazine.com/2020/08/20/marley-dias-black-girl-books-1000blackgirlbooks-a-push-for-representation-in-childrens-literature/ on February 28, 2022.

Schwartz, S. (2021, February 3). Lawmakers push to ban '1619 Project' from schools. *Education Week*. Accessed at www.edweek.org/teaching-learning/lawmakers-push-to-ban-1619-project-from-schools/2021/02 on December 6, 2021.

Schweitzer, A. (2021, June 22). *The D.C. region has become more diverse – but also more segregated, study finds*. Accessed at www.npr.org/local/305/2021/06/22/1009054384/the-d-c-region-has-become-more-diverse-but-also-more-segregated-study-finds on October 21, 2021.

Sesame Street. (n.d.). *Skin song* [Video file]. Accessed at www.youtube.com/watch?v=uy5F2hMNC9M on August 9, 2021.

Sesame Street. (2010, October 12). *I love my hair* [Video file]. Accessed at www.youtube.com/watch?v=enpFde5rgmw on August 9, 2021.

Sesame Street. (2011, October 14). *Mark Ruffalo: Empathy* [Video file]. Accessed at www.youtube.com/watch?v=9_1Rt1R4xbM on August 9, 2021.

Sesame Street. (2014a, September 17). *Beautiful skin song* [Video file]. Accessed at www.youtube.com/watch?v=oq9ydJK6Fn8 on August 9, 2021.

Sesame Street. (2014b, September 10). *Janelle Monáe—Power of yet* [Video file]. Accessed at www.youtube.com/watch?v=XLeUvZvuvAs on August 3, 2021.

Sesame Street. (2014c, September 10). *Lupita Nyong'o loves her skin* [Video file]. Accessed at www.youtube.com/watch?v=xIC2hHECZ6Y on August 9, 2021.

Silverstein, J. (2019, December 19). Why we published the 1619 Project. *The New York Times*. Accessed at www.nytimes.com/interactive/2019/12/20/magazine/1619-intro.html on August 6, 2021.

Smooth, J. (2011, November 15). *How I learned to stop worrying and love talking about race* [Video file]. Accessed at www.youtube.com/watch?v=MbdxeFcQtaU on August 6, 2021.

Social Justice Books. (2017). *Selecting and rating titles for social justice*. Accessed at https://socialjusticebooks.org/selecting-and-rating-titles-for-social-justice-books/ on August 5, 2021.

Southern Education Foundation. (2016). *Race and ethnicity in a new era of private funding of public schools: Private school enrollment in the South and the nation.* Atlanta, GA: Author. Accessed at southerneducation.org on March 21, 2022.

Staats, C. (2013). *State of the science: Implicit bias review.* Columbus, OH: Kirwan Institute. Accessed at http://kirwaninstitute.osu.edu/implicit-bias-training/resources/2013-implicit-bias-review.pdf on August 6, 2021.

Stamberg, S. (2017, March 28). *Kerry James Marshall: A Black presence in the art world is "not negotiable."* Accessed at www.npr.org/2017/03/28/521683667/kerry-james-marshall-a-black-presence-in-the-art-world-is-not-negotiable on August 6, 2021.

Steele, C. M. (2011). *Whistling Vivaldi: How stereotypes affect us and what we can do.* New York: W. W. Norton.

Steele, D. M., & Cohn-Vargas, B. (2013). *Identity safe classrooms, grades K–5: Places to belong and learn.* Thousand Oaks, CA: Corwin Press.

Stevenson, B. (2014). *Just mercy: A story of justice and redemption.* New York: Random House.

Stevenson, H. C. (2014). *Promoting racial literacy in schools: Differences that make a difference.* New York: Teachers College Press.

Strauss, R. (2013). *Tree of life: The incredible biodiversity of life on Earth.* Tonawanda, NY: Kids Can Press.

Strauss, V. (2021, June 12). Teachers across the country protest laws restricting lessons on racism. *The Washington Post.* Accessed at www.washingtonpost.com/education/2021/06/12/teachers-protest-laws-restricting-antiracism-lessons-in-school/ on December 16, 2021.

Sue, D. W., Capodilupo, C. M., Torino, G. C., Bucceri, J. M., Holder, A. M. B., Nadal, K. L., et al. (2007). Racial microaggressions in everyday life: Implications for clinical practice. *American Psychologist, 62*(4), 271–286.

Sullivan, J. N., Eberhardt, J. L., & Roberts, S. O. (2021). Conversations about race in black and white US families: Before and after George Floyd's death. *Proceedings of the National Academy of Sciences, 118*(38).

Swain-Bates, C. (2013). *Big hair, don't care.* Atlanta, GA: Goldest Karat Publishing.

Tarpley, N. A. (2001). *I love my hair!* Boston: Little, Brown.

Tatum, B. D. (1992). Talking about race, learning about racism: The application of racial identity development theory in the classroom. *Harvard Educational Review, 62*(1), 1–24. Accessed at https://equity.ucla.edu/wp-content/uploads/2017/01/Tatum-Talking-About-Race.pdf on August 9, 2021.

Tatum, B. D. (1994). Teaching White students about racism: The search for White allies and the restoration of hope. *Teachers College Record, 95*(4), 462–476. Accessed at www.goldenbridgesschool.org/uploads/1/9/5/4/19541249/teaching_white_students_about_racism.pdf on August 9, 2021.

Tatum, B. D. (2017). *Why are all the Black kids sitting together in the cafeteria? And other conversations about race* (2nd ed.). New York: Basic Books.

Taub, A. (2016, November 2). Behind the gathering turmoil, a crisis of White identity. *The New York Times.* Accessed at www.nytimes.com/2016/11/02/world/americas/brexit-donald-trump-whites.html on August 9, 2021.

Teaching for Change. (n.d.). *What we do.* Accessed at www.teachingforchange.org/about/what-we-do on November 11, 2021.

Theoharis, J. (2021, February 1). The real Rosa Parks story is better than the fairy tale. *The New York Times.* Accessed at www.nytimes.com/2021/02/01/opinion/rosa-parks.html on January 31, 2022.

TIME Staff. (2020, July 6). *21 lessons from America's worst moments.* Accessed at https://time.com/5858169/americas-worst-moments/ on August 9, 2021.

Tochluk, S. (2010). *Witnessing whiteness: The need to talk about race and how to do it* (2nd ed.). Lanham, MD: Rowman & Littlefield.

Tyler, M. (2005). *The skin you live in.* Chicago: Chicago Children's Museum.

Udry, J. M. (1987). *A tree is nice.* New York: HarperCollins.

USC Rossier School of Education. (2021). *Why conversations about racism belong in the classroom.* Accessed at https://rossieronline.usc.edu/youth-and-racism/racism-in-the-classroom on October 8, 2021.

Vittrup, B. (2016). Colorblind or color conscious? White American mothers' approaches to racial socialization. *Journal of Family Issues, 39*(3), 668–692.

Vygotsky, L. S. (1978). *Mind in society: The development of higher psychological processes.* Cambridge, MA: Harvard University Press.

Wagner, T. (2008). *The global achievement gap: Why even our best schools don't teach the new survival skills our children need—and what we can do about it.* New York: Basic Books.

Watanabe, T. (2005, February 5). A lifelong lesson in justice. *Los Angeles Times.* Accessed at latimes.com/archives/la-xpm-2005-feb-05-me-teachers5-story.html on August 4, 2021.

Watson, R. (2012). *Harlem's little blackbird: The story of Florence Mills.* New York: Random House.

Wilkerson, I. (2020). *Caste: The origins of our discontents.* New York: Random House.

Will, M. (2020, April 14). Still mostly White and female: New federal data on the teaching profession. *Education Week.* Accessed at www.edweek.org/leadership/still-mostly-white-and-female-new-federal-data-on-the-teaching-profession/2020/04 on August 9, 2021.

Williamson, V., & Gelfand, I. (2019, August 14). *Trump and racism: What do the data say?* [Blog post]. Accessed at www.brookings.edu/blog/fixgov/2019/08/14/trump-and-racism-what-do-the-data-say/ on November 1, 2021.

Wingfield, A. H. (2015, September 13). Color blindness is counterproductive. *The Atlantic.* Accessed at www.theatlantic.com/politics/archive/2015/09/color-blindness-is-counterproductive/405037/ on November 1, 2021.

Winkler, E. N. (2009). Children are not colorblind: How young children learn race. *PACE, 3*(3), 1–8. Accessed at https://inclusions.org/wp-content/uploads/2017/11/Children-are-Not-Colorblind.pdf on August 9, 2021.

Winkler, E. N. (2012). *Learning race, learning place: Shaping racial identities and ideas in African American childhoods.* New Brunswick, NJ: Rutgers University Press.

Winter, J. (2018). *Wangari's trees of peace: A true story from Africa*. Boston: Clarion Books.

Wise, T. (2011). *White like me: Reflections on race from a privileged son*. New York: Soft Skull Press.

Wise, T. (2012). *Dear White America: Letter to a new minority.* San Francisco: City Lights Books.

Woodson, J. (2018). *The day you begin.* New York: Nancy Paulsen Books.

Wright, J. (2021, February 16). *Jumpstart your heart with a "Daly" dose of healthy foods* [Blog post]. Accessed at www.usda.gov/media/blog/2021/02/16/jumpstart-your-heart-daly-dose-healthy-foods on December 13, 2021.

Xavier, J. (2016, July 15). *How racial threat has galvanized the Tea Party.* Accessed at www.gsb.stanford.edu/insights/how-racial-threat-has-galvanized-tea-party on August 9, 2021.

Xiao, N. G., Quinn, P. C., Liu, S., Ge, L., Pascalis, O., & Lee, K. (2017). Older but not younger infants associate own-race faces with happy music and other-race faces with sad music. *Developmental Science, 21*(2).

Zhang, Z. (2014, November 6). *Author of* Whistling Vivaldi *discusses "stereotype threat."* Accessed at www.thecrimson.com/article/2014/11/6/steele-stereotype-threat-harvard/ on October 20, 2021.

Zinn, H., & Arnove, A. (2015). *A people's history of the United States* (35th anniversary ed.). New York: Harper Perennial.

Zonta, M. (2019, July 15). *Racial disparities in home appreciation.* Accessed at www.americanprogress.org/issues/economy/reports/2019/07/15/469838/racial-disparities-home-appreciation/ on August 9, 2021.

Zou, I. (2021, August 24). *"I wanted to teach differently than I had been taught": How some Texas educators practice anti-racist teaching.* Accessed at www.kristv.com/news/texas-news/i-wanted-to-teach-differently-than-i-had-been-taught-how-some-texas-educators-practice-anti-racist-teaching on December 16, 2021.

INDEX

C

D

E

Q

R

S

Y

Z